C-2230   CAREER EXAMINATION SERIES

This is your
PASSBOOK for...

Fire Safety Officer

Test Preparation Study Guide
Questions & Answers

COPYRIGHT NOTICE

This book is SOLELY intended for, is sold ONLY to, and its use is RESTRICTED to individual, bona fide applicants or candidates who qualify by virtue of having seriously filed applications for appropriate license, certificate, professional and/or promotional advancement, higher school matriculation, scholarship, or other legitimate requirements of education and/or governmental authorities.

This book is NOT intended for use, class instruction, tutoring, training, duplication, copying, reprinting, excerption, or adaptation, etc., by:

1) Other publishers
2) Proprietors and/or Instructors of "Coaching" and/or Preparatory Courses
3) Personnel and/or Training Divisions of commercial, industrial, and governmental organizations
4) Schools, colleges, or universities and/or their departments and staffs, including teachers and other personnel
5) Testing Agencies or Bureaus
6) Study groups which seek by the purchase of a single volume to copy and/or duplicate and/or adapt this material for use by the group as a whole without having purchased individual volumes for each of the members of the group
7) Et al.

Such persons would be in violation of appropriate Federal and State statutes.

PROVISION OF LICENSING AGREEMENTS – Recognized educational, commercial, industrial, and governmental institutions and organizations, and others legitimately engaged in educational pursuits, including training, testing, and measurement activities, may address request for a licensing agreement to the copyright owners, who will determine whether, and under what conditions, including fees and charges, the materials in this book may be used them. In other words, a licensing facility exists for the legitimate use of the material in this book on other than an individual basis. However, it is asseverated and affirmed here that the material in this book CANNOT be used without the receipt of the express permission of such a licensing agreement from the Publishers. Inquiries re licensing should be addressed to the company, attention rights and permissions department.

All rights reserved, including the right of reproduction in whole or in part, in any form or by any means, electronic or mechanical, including photocopying, recording, or by any information storage and retrieval system, without permission in writing from the Publisher.

Copyright © 2025 by
National Learning Corporation

212 Michael Drive, Syosset, NY 11791
(516) 921-8888 • www.passbooks.com
E-mail: info@passbooks.com

PASSBOOK® SERIES

THE *PASSBOOK® SERIES* has been created to prepare applicants and candidates for the ultimate academic battlefield – the examination room.

At some time in our lives, each and every one of us may be required to take an examination – for validation, matriculation, admission, qualification, registration, certification, or licensure.

Based on the assumption that every applicant or candidate has met the basic formal educational standards, has taken the required number of courses, and read the necessary texts, the *PASSBOOK® SERIES* furnishes the one special preparation which may assure passing with confidence, instead of failing with insecurity. Examination questions – together with answers – are furnished as the basic vehicle for study so that the mysteries of the examination and its compounding difficulties may be eliminated or diminished by a sure method.

This book is meant to help you pass your examination provided that you qualify and are serious in your objective.

The entire field is reviewed through the huge store of content information which is succinctly presented through a provocative and challenging approach – the question-and-answer method.

A climate of success is established by furnishing the correct answers at the end of each test.

You soon learn to recognize types of questions, forms of questions, and patterns of questioning. You may even begin to anticipate expected outcomes.

You perceive that many questions are repeated or adapted so that you can gain acute insights, which may enable you to score many sure points.

You learn how to confront new questions, or types of questions, and to attack them confidently and work out the correct answers.

You note objectives and emphases, and recognize pitfalls and dangers, so that you may make positive educational adjustments.

Moreover, you are kept fully informed in relation to new concepts, methods, practices, and directions in the field.

You discover that you are actually taking the examination all the time: you are preparing for the examination by "taking" an examination, not by reading extraneous and/or supererogatory textbooks.

In short, this PASSBOOK®, used directedly, should be an important factor in helping you to pass your test.

FIRE SAFETY OFFICER

DUTIES
Inspects buildings to determine where fire hazards exist and makes recommendations for correction of unsafe conditions; plans and develops fire safety and fire prevention programs for presentation to various groups; investigates the nature and cause of fires; researches new methods, techniques, and products of the fire service; perform related duties.

SCOPE OF THE WRITTEN TEST
The written test will be designed to cover knowledges, skills, and/or abilities in the following areas:
1. Fire prevention, including fire inspections and fire hazards;
2. Fire investigation techniques and fire behavior characteristics;
3. Understanding and interpreting fire prevention laws and codes; and
4. Preparation of written material.

HOW TO TAKE A TEST

I. YOU MUST PASS AN EXAMINATION

A. *WHAT EVERY CANDIDATE SHOULD KNOW*

Examination applicants often ask us for help in preparing for the written test. What can I study in advance? What kinds of questions will be asked? How will the test be given? How will the papers be graded?

As an applicant for a civil service examination, you may be wondering about some of these things. Our purpose here is to suggest effective methods of advance study and to describe civil service examinations.

Your chances for success on this examination can be increased if you know how to prepare. Those "pre-examination jitters" can be reduced if you know what to expect. You can even experience an adventure in good citizenship if you know why civil service exams are given.

B. *WHY ARE CIVIL SERVICE EXAMINATIONS GIVEN?*

Civil service examinations are important to you in two ways. As a citizen, you want public jobs filled by employees who know how to do their work. As a job seeker, you want a fair chance to compete for that job on an equal footing with other candidates. The best-known means of accomplishing this two-fold goal is the competitive examination.

Exams are widely publicized throughout the nation. They may be administered for jobs in federal, state, city, municipal, town or village governments or agencies.

Any citizen may apply, with some limitations, such as the age or residence of applicants. Your experience and education may be reviewed to see whether you meet the requirements for the particular examination. When these requirements exist, they are reasonable and applied consistently to all applicants. Thus, a competitive examination may cause you some uneasiness now, but it is your privilege and safeguard.

C. *HOW ARE CIVIL SERVICE EXAMS DEVELOPED?*

Examinations are carefully written by trained technicians who are specialists in the field known as "psychological measurement," in consultation with recognized authorities in the field of work that the test will cover. These experts recommend the subject matter areas or skills to be tested; only those knowledges or skills important to your success on the job are included. The most reliable books and source materials available are used as references. Together, the experts and technicians judge the difficulty level of the questions.

Test technicians know how to phrase questions so that the problem is clearly stated. Their ethics do not permit "trick" or "catch" questions. Questions may have been tried out on sample groups, or subjected to statistical analysis, to determine their usefulness.

Written tests are often used in combination with performance tests, ratings of training and experience, and oral interviews. All of these measures combine to form the best-known means of finding the right person for the right job.

II. HOW TO PASS THE WRITTEN TEST

A. NATURE OF THE EXAMINATION

To prepare intelligently for civil service examinations, you should know how they differ from school examinations you have taken. In school you were assigned certain definite pages to read or subjects to cover. The examination questions were quite detailed and usually emphasized memory. Civil service exams, on the other hand, try to discover your present ability to perform the duties of a position, plus your potentiality to learn these duties. In other words, a civil service exam attempts to predict how successful you will be. Questions cover such a broad area that they cannot be as minute and detailed as school exam questions.

In the public service similar kinds of work, or positions, are grouped together in one "class." This process is known as *position-classification*. All the positions in a class are paid according to the salary range for that class. One class title covers all of these positions, and they are all tested by the same examination.

B. FOUR BASIC STEPS

1) Study the announcement

How, then, can you know what subjects to study? Our best answer is: "Learn as much as possible about the class of positions for which you've applied." The exam will test the knowledge, skills and abilities needed to do the work.

Your most valuable source of information about the position you want is the official exam announcement. This announcement lists the training and experience qualifications. Check these standards and apply only if you come reasonably close to meeting them.

The brief description of the position in the examination announcement offers some clues to the subjects which will be tested. Think about the job itself. Review the duties in your mind. Can you perform them, or are there some in which you are rusty? Fill in the blank spots in your preparation.

Many jurisdictions preview the written test in the exam announcement by including a section called "Knowledge and Abilities Required," "Scope of the Examination," or some similar heading. Here you will find out specifically what fields will be tested.

2) Review your own background

Once you learn in general what the position is all about, and what you need to know to do the work, ask yourself which subjects you already know fairly well and which need improvement. You may wonder whether to concentrate on improving your strong areas or on building some background in your fields of weakness. When the announcement has specified "some knowledge" or "considerable knowledge," or has used adjectives like "beginning principles of..." or "advanced ... methods," you can get a clue as to the number and difficulty of questions to be asked in any given field. More questions, and hence broader coverage, would be included for those subjects which are more important in the work. Now weigh your strengths and weaknesses against the job requirements and prepare accordingly.

3) Determine the level of the position

Another way to tell how intensively you should prepare is to understand the level of the job for which you are applying. Is it the entering level? In other words, is this the position in which beginners in a field of work are hired? Or is it an intermediate or advanced level? Sometimes this is indicated by such words as "Junior" or "Senior" in the class title. Other jurisdictions use Roman numerals to designate the level – Clerk I, Clerk II, for example. The word "Supervisor" sometimes appears in the title. If the level is not indicated by the title, check the description of duties. Will you be working under very close supervision, or will you have responsibility for independent decisions in this work?

4) Choose appropriate study materials

Now that you know the subjects to be examined and the relative amount of each subject to be covered, you can choose suitable study materials. For beginning level jobs, or even advanced ones, if you have a pronounced weakness in some aspect of your training, read a modern, standard textbook in that field. Be sure it is up to date and has general coverage. Such books are normally available at your library, and the librarian will be glad to help you locate one. For entry-level positions, questions of appropriate difficulty are chosen – neither highly advanced questions, nor those too simple. Such questions require careful thought but not advanced training.

If the position for which you are applying is technical or advanced, you will read more advanced, specialized material. If you are already familiar with the basic principles of your field, elementary textbooks would waste your time. Concentrate on advanced textbooks and technical periodicals. Think through the concepts and review difficult problems in your field.

These are all general sources. You can get more ideas on your own initiative, following these leads. For example, training manuals and publications of the government agency which employs workers in your field can be useful, particularly for technical and professional positions. A letter or visit to the government department involved may result in more specific study suggestions, and certainly will provide you with a more definite idea of the exact nature of the position you are seeking.

III. KINDS OF TESTS

Tests are used for purposes other than measuring knowledge and ability to perform specified duties. For some positions, it is equally important to test ability to make adjustments to new situations or to profit from training. In others, basic mental abilities not dependent on information are essential. Questions which test these things may not appear as pertinent to the duties of the position as those which test for knowledge and information. Yet they are often highly important parts of a fair examination. For very general questions, it is almost impossible to help you direct your study efforts. What we can do is to point out some of the more common of these general abilities needed in public service positions and describe some typical questions.

1) General information

Broad, general information has been found useful for predicting job success in some kinds of work. This is tested in a variety of ways, from vocabulary lists to questions about current events. Basic background in some field of work, such as sociology or economics, may be sampled in a group of questions. Often these are principles which have become familiar to most persons through exposure rather than through formal training. It is difficult to advise you how to study for these questions; being alert to the world around you is our best suggestion.

2) Verbal ability

An example of an ability needed in many positions is verbal or language ability. Verbal ability is, in brief, the ability to use and understand words. Vocabulary and grammar tests are typical measures of this ability. Reading comprehension or paragraph interpretation questions are common in many kinds of civil service tests. You are given a paragraph of written material and asked to find its central meaning.

3) Numerical ability

Number skills can be tested by the familiar arithmetic problem, by checking paired lists of numbers to see which are alike and which are different, or by interpreting charts and graphs. In the latter test, a graph may be printed in the test booklet which you are asked to use as the basis for answering questions.

4) Observation

A popular test for law-enforcement positions is the observation test. A picture is shown to you for several minutes, then taken away. Questions about the picture test your ability to observe both details and larger elements.

5) Following directions

In many positions in the public service, the employee must be able to carry out written instructions dependably and accurately. You may be given a chart with several columns, each column listing a variety of information. The questions require you to carry out directions involving the information given in the chart.

6) Skills and aptitudes

Performance tests effectively measure some manual skills and aptitudes. When the skill is one in which you are trained, such as typing or shorthand, you can practice. These tests are often very much like those given in business school or high school courses. For many of the other skills and aptitudes, however, no short-time preparation can be made. Skills and abilities natural to you or that you have developed throughout your lifetime are being tested.

Many of the general questions just described provide all the data needed to answer the questions and ask you to use your reasoning ability to find the answers. Your best preparation for these tests, as well as for tests of facts and ideas, is to be at your physical and mental best. You, no doubt, have your own methods of getting into an exam-taking mood and keeping "in shape." The next section lists some ideas on this subject.

IV. KINDS OF QUESTIONS

Only rarely is the "essay" question, which you answer in narrative form, used in civil service tests. Civil service tests are usually of the short-answer type. Full instructions for answering these questions will be given to you at the examination. But in case this is your first experience with short-answer questions and separate answer sheets, here is what you need to know:

1) Multiple-choice Questions

Most popular of the short-answer questions is the "multiple choice" or "best answer" question. It can be used, for example, to test for factual knowledge, ability to solve problems or judgment in meeting situations found at work.

A multiple-choice question is normally one of three types—
- It can begin with an incomplete statement followed by several possible endings. You are to find the one ending which *best* completes the statement, although some of the others may not be entirely wrong.
- It can also be a complete statement in the form of a question which is answered by choosing one of the statements listed.

- It can be in the form of a problem – again you select the best answer.

Here is an example of a multiple-choice question with a discussion which should give you some clues as to the method for choosing the right answer:

When an employee has a complaint about his assignment, the action which will *best* help him overcome his difficulty is to
- A. discuss his difficulty with his coworkers
- B. take the problem to the head of the organization
- C. take the problem to the person who gave him the assignment
- D. say nothing to anyone about his complaint

In answering this question, you should study each of the choices to find which is best. Consider choice "A" – Certainly an employee may discuss his complaint with fellow employees, but no change or improvement can result, and the complaint remains unresolved. Choice "B" is a poor choice since the head of the organization probably does not know what assignment you have been given, and taking your problem to him is known as "going over the head" of the supervisor. The supervisor, or person who made the assignment, is the person who can clarify it or correct any injustice. Choice "C" is, therefore, correct. To say nothing, as in choice "D," is unwise. Supervisors have and interest in knowing the problems employees are facing, and the employee is seeking a solution to his problem.

2) True/False Questions

The "true/false" or "right/wrong" form of question is sometimes used. Here a complete statement is given. Your job is to decide whether the statement is right or wrong.

SAMPLE: A roaming cell-phone call to a nearby city costs less than a non-roaming call to a distant city.

This statement is wrong, or false, since roaming calls are more expensive.

This is not a complete list of all possible question forms, although most of the others are variations of these common types. You will always get complete directions for answering questions. Be sure you understand *how* to mark your answers – ask questions until you do.

V. RECORDING YOUR ANSWERS

Computer terminals are used more and more today for many different kinds of exams.

For an examination with very few applicants, you may be told to record your answers in the test booklet itself. Separate answer sheets are much more common. If this separate answer sheet is to be scored by machine – and this is often the case – it is highly important that you mark your answers correctly in order to get credit.

An electronic scoring machine is often used in civil service offices because of the speed with which papers can be scored. Machine-scored answer sheets must be marked with a pencil, which will be given to you. This pencil has a high graphite content which responds to the electronic scoring machine. As a matter of fact, stray dots may register as answers, so do not let your pencil rest on the answer sheet while you are pondering the correct answer. Also, if your pencil lead breaks or is otherwise defective, ask for another.

Since the answer sheet will be dropped in a slot in the scoring machine, be careful not to bend the corners or get the paper crumpled.

The answer sheet normally has five vertical columns of numbers, with 30 numbers to a column. These numbers correspond to the question numbers in your test booklet. After each number, going across the page are four or five pairs of dotted lines. These short dotted lines have small letters or numbers above them. The first two pairs may also have a "T" or "F" above the letters. This indicates that the first two pairs only are to be used if the questions are of the true-false type. If the questions are multiple choice, disregard the "T" and "F" and pay attention only to the small letters or numbers.

Answer your questions in the manner of the sample that follows:

32. The largest city in the United States is
    A. Washington, D.C.
    B. New York City
    C. Chicago
    D. Detroit
    E. San Francisco

1) Choose the answer you think is best. (New York City is the largest, so "B" is correct.)
2) Find the row of dotted lines numbered the same as the question you are answering. (Find row number 32)
3) Find the pair of dotted lines corresponding to the answer. (Find the pair of lines under the mark "B.")
4) Make a solid black mark between the dotted lines.

VI. BEFORE THE TEST

Common sense will help you find procedures to follow to get ready for an examination. Too many of us, however, overlook these sensible measures. Indeed, nervousness and fatigue have been found to be the most serious reasons why applicants fail to do their best on civil service tests. Here is a list of reminders:

- Begin your preparation early – Don't wait until the last minute to go scurrying around for books and materials or to find out what the position is all about.
- Prepare continuously – An hour a night for a week is better than an all-night cram session. This has been definitely established. What is more, a night a week for a month will return better dividends than crowding your study into a shorter period of time.
- Locate the place of the exam – You have been sent a notice telling you when and where to report for the examination. If the location is in a different town or otherwise unfamiliar to you, it would be well to inquire the best route and learn something about the building.
- Relax the night before the test – Allow your mind to rest. Do not study at all that night. Plan some mild recreation or diversion; then go to bed early and get a good night's sleep.
- Get up early enough to make a leisurely trip to the place for the test – This way unforeseen events, traffic snarls, unfamiliar buildings, etc. will not upset you.
- Dress comfortably – A written test is not a fashion show. You will be known by number and not by name, so wear something comfortable.

- Leave excess paraphernalia at home – Shopping bags and odd bundles will get in your way. You need bring only the items mentioned in the official notice you received; usually everything you need is provided. Do not bring reference books to the exam. They will only confuse those last minutes and be taken away from you when in the test room.
- Arrive somewhat ahead of time – If because of transportation schedules you must get there very early, bring a newspaper or magazine to take your mind off yourself while waiting.
- Locate the examination room – When you have found the proper room, you will be directed to the seat or part of the room where you will sit. Sometimes you are given a sheet of instructions to read while you are waiting. Do not fill out any forms until you are told to do so; just read them and be prepared.
- Relax and prepare to listen to the instructions
- If you have any physical problem that may keep you from doing your best, be sure to tell the test administrator. If you are sick or in poor health, you really cannot do your best on the exam. You can come back and take the test some other time.

VII. AT THE TEST

The day of the test is here and you have the test booklet in your hand. The temptation to get going is very strong. Caution! There is more to success than knowing the right answers. You must know how to identify your papers and understand variations in the type of short-answer question used in this particular examination. Follow these suggestions for maximum results from your efforts:

1) Cooperate with the monitor

The test administrator has a duty to create a situation in which you can be as much at ease as possible. He will give instructions, tell you when to begin, check to see that you are marking your answer sheet correctly, and so on. He is not there to guard you, although he will see that your competitors do not take unfair advantage. He wants to help you do your best.

2) Listen to all instructions

Don't jump the gun! Wait until you understand all directions. In most civil service tests you get more time than you need to answer the questions. So don't be in a hurry. Read each word of instructions until you clearly understand the meaning. Study the examples, listen to all announcements and follow directions. Ask questions if you do not understand what to do.

3) Identify your papers

Civil service exams are usually identified by number only. You will be assigned a number; you must not put your name on your test papers. Be sure to copy your number correctly. Since more than one exam may be given, copy your exact examination title.

4) Plan your time

Unless you are told that a test is a "speed" or "rate of work" test, speed itself is usually not important. Time enough to answer all the questions will be provided, but this does not mean that you have all day. An overall time limit has been set. Divide the total time (in minutes) by the number of questions to determine the approximate time you have for each question.

5) Do not linger over difficult questions

If you come across a difficult question, mark it with a paper clip (useful to have along) and come back to it when you have been through the booklet. One caution if you do this – be sure to skip a number on your answer sheet as well. Check often to be sure that you have not lost your place and that you are marking in the row numbered the same as the question you are answering.

6) Read the questions

Be sure you know what the question asks! Many capable people are unsuccessful because they failed to *read* the questions correctly.

7) Answer all questions

Unless you have been instructed that a penalty will be deducted for incorrect answers, it is better to guess than to omit a question.

8) Speed tests

It is often better NOT to guess on speed tests. It has been found that on timed tests people are tempted to spend the last few seconds before time is called in marking answers at random – without even reading them – in the hope of picking up a few extra points. To discourage this practice, the instructions may warn you that your score will be "corrected" for guessing. That is, a penalty will be applied. The incorrect answers will be deducted from the correct ones, or some other penalty formula will be used.

9) Review your answers

If you finish before time is called, go back to the questions you guessed or omitted to give them further thought. Review other answers if you have time.

10) Return your test materials

If you are ready to leave before others have finished or time is called, take ALL your materials to the monitor and leave quietly. Never take any test material with you. The monitor can discover whose papers are not complete, and taking a test booklet may be grounds for disqualification.

VIII. EXAMINATION TECHNIQUES

1) Read the general instructions carefully. These are usually printed on the first page of the exam booklet. As a rule, these instructions refer to the timing of the examination; the fact that you should not start work until the signal and must stop work at a signal, etc. If there are any *special* instructions, such as a choice of questions to be answered, make sure that you note this instruction carefully.

2) When you are ready to start work on the examination, that is as soon as the signal has been given, read the instructions to each question booklet, underline any key words or phrases, such as *least, best, outline, describe* and the like. In this way you will tend to answer as requested rather than discover on reviewing your paper that you *listed without describing*, that you selected the *worst* choice rather than the *best* choice, etc.

3) If the examination is of the objective or multiple-choice type – that is, each question will also give a series of possible answers: A, B, C or D, and you are called upon to select the best answer and write the letter next to that answer on your answer paper – it is advisable to start answering each question in turn. There may be anywhere from 50 to 100 such questions in the three or four hours allotted and you can see how much time would be taken if you read through all the questions before beginning to answer any. Furthermore, if you come across a question or group of questions which you know would be difficult to answer, it would undoubtedly affect your handling of all the other questions.

4) If the examination is of the essay type and contains but a few questions, it is a moot point as to whether you should read all the questions before starting to answer any one. Of course, if you are given a choice – say five out of seven and the like – then it is essential to read all the questions so you can eliminate the two that are most difficult. If, however, you are asked to answer all the questions, there may be danger in trying to answer the easiest one first because you may find that you will spend too much time on it. The best technique is to answer the first question, then proceed to the second, etc.

5) Time your answers. Before the exam begins, write down the time it started, then add the time allowed for the examination and write down the time it must be completed, then divide the time available somewhat as follows:
    - If 3-1/2 hours are allowed, that would be 210 minutes. If you have 80 objective-type questions, that would be an average of 2-1/2 minutes per question. Allow yourself no more than 2 minutes per question, or a total of 160 minutes, which will permit about 50 minutes to review.
    - If for the time allotment of 210 minutes there are 7 essay questions to answer, that would average about 30 minutes a question. Give yourself only 25 minutes per question so that you have about 35 minutes to review.

6) The most important instruction is to *read each question* and make sure you know what is wanted. The second most important instruction is to *time yourself properly* so that you answer every question. The third most important instruction is to *answer every question*. Guess if you have to but include something for each question. Remember that you will receive no credit for a blank and will probably receive some credit if you write something in answer to an essay question. If you guess a letter – say "B" for a multiple-choice question – you may have guessed right. If you leave a blank as an answer to a multiple-choice question, the examiners may respect your feelings but it will not add a point to your score. Some exams may penalize you for wrong answers, so in such cases *only*, you may not want to guess unless you have some basis for your answer.

7) Suggestions
    a. Objective-type questions
        1. Examine the question booklet for proper sequence of pages and questions
        2. Read all instructions carefully
        3. Skip any question which seems too difficult; return to it after all other questions have been answered
        4. Apportion your time properly; do not spend too much time on any single question or group of questions

5. Note and underline key words – *all, most, fewest, least, best, worst, same, opposite,* etc.
6. Pay particular attention to negatives
7. Note unusual option, e.g., unduly long, short, complex, different or similar in content to the body of the question
8. Observe the use of "hedging" words – *probably, may, most likely,* etc.
9. Make sure that your answer is put next to the same number as the question
10. Do not second-guess unless you have good reason to believe the second answer is definitely more correct
11. Cross out original answer if you decide another answer is more accurate; do not erase until you are ready to hand your paper in
12. Answer all questions; guess unless instructed otherwise
13. Leave time for review

   b. Essay questions
1. Read each question carefully
2. Determine exactly what is wanted. Underline key words or phrases.
3. Decide on outline or paragraph answer
4. Include many different points and elements unless asked to develop any one or two points or elements
5. Show impartiality by giving pros and cons unless directed to select one side only
6. Make and write down any assumptions you find necessary to answer the questions
7. Watch your English, grammar, punctuation and choice of words
8. Time your answers; don't crowd material

8) Answering the essay question

Most essay questions can be answered by framing the specific response around several key words or ideas. Here are a few such key words or ideas:

M's: manpower, materials, methods, money, management
P's: purpose, program, policy, plan, procedure, practice, problems, pitfalls, personnel, public relations

   a. Six basic steps in handling problems:
1. Preliminary plan and background development
2. Collect information, data and facts
3. Analyze and interpret information, data and facts
4. Analyze and develop solutions as well as make recommendations
5. Prepare report and sell recommendations
6. Install recommendations and follow up effectiveness

   b. Pitfalls to avoid
1. *Taking things for granted* – A statement of the situation does not necessarily imply that each of the elements is necessarily true; for example, a complaint may be invalid and biased so that all that can be taken for granted is that a complaint has been registered

2. *Considering only one side of a situation* – Wherever possible, indicate several alternatives and then point out the reasons you selected the best one
3. *Failing to indicate follow up* – Whenever your answer indicates action on your part, make certain that you will take proper follow-up action to see how successful your recommendations, procedures or actions turn out to be
4. *Taking too long in answering any single question* – Remember to time your answers properly

IX. AFTER THE TEST

Scoring procedures differ in detail among civil service jurisdictions although the general principles are the same. Whether the papers are hand-scored or graded by machine we have described, they are nearly always graded by number. That is, the person who marks the paper knows only the number – never the name – of the applicant. Not until all the papers have been graded will they be matched with names. If other tests, such as training and experience or oral interview ratings have been given, scores will be combined. Different parts of the examination usually have different weights. For example, the written test might count 60 percent of the final grade, and a rating of training and experience 40 percent. In many jurisdictions, veterans will have a certain number of points added to their grades.

After the final grade has been determined, the names are placed in grade order and an eligible list is established. There are various methods for resolving ties between those who get the same final grade – probably the most common is to place first the name of the person whose application was received first. Job offers are made from the eligible list in the order the names appear on it. You will be notified of your grade and your rank as soon as all these computations have been made. This will be done as rapidly as possible.

People who are found to meet the requirements in the announcement are called "eligibles." Their names are put on a list of eligible candidates. An eligible's chances of getting a job depend on how high he stands on this list and how fast agencies are filling jobs from the list.

When a job is to be filled from a list of eligibles, the agency asks for the names of people on the list of eligibles for that job. When the civil service commission receives this request, it sends to the agency the names of the three people highest on this list. Or, if the job to be filled has specialized requirements, the office sends the agency the names of the top three persons who meet these requirements from the general list.

The appointing officer makes a choice from among the three people whose names were sent to him. If the selected person accepts the appointment, the names of the others are put back on the list to be considered for future openings.

That is the rule in hiring from all kinds of eligible lists, whether they are for typist, carpenter, chemist, or something else. For every vacancy, the appointing officer has his choice of any one of the top three eligibles on the list. This explains why the person whose name is on top of the list sometimes does not get an appointment when some of the persons lower on the list do. If the appointing officer chooses the second or third eligible, the No. 1 eligible does not get a job at once, but stays on the list until he is appointed or the list is terminated.

X. HOW TO PASS THE INTERVIEW TEST

The examination for which you applied requires an oral interview test. You have already taken the written test and you are now being called for the interview test – the final part of the formal examination.

You may think that it is not possible to prepare for an interview test and that there are no procedures to follow during an interview. Our purpose is to point out some things you can do in advance that will help you and some good rules to follow and pitfalls to avoid while you are being interviewed.

What is an interview supposed to test?

The written examination is designed to test the technical knowledge and competence of the candidate; the oral is designed to evaluate intangible qualities, not readily measured otherwise, and to establish a list showing the relative fitness of each candidate – as measured against his competitors – for the position sought. Scoring is not on the basis of "right" and "wrong," but on a sliding scale of values ranging from "not passable" to "outstanding." As a matter of fact, it is possible to achieve a relatively low score without a single "incorrect" answer because of evident weakness in the qualities being measured.

Occasionally, an examination may consist entirely of an oral test – either an individual or a group oral. In such cases, information is sought concerning the technical knowledges and abilities of the candidate, since there has been no written examination for this purpose. More commonly, however, an oral test is used to supplement a written examination.

Who conducts interviews?

The composition of oral boards varies among different jurisdictions. In nearly all, a representative of the personnel department serves as chairman. One of the members of the board may be a representative of the department in which the candidate would work. In some cases, "outside experts" are used, and, frequently, a businessman or some other representative of the general public is asked to serve. Labor and management or other special groups may be represented. The aim is to secure the services of experts in the appropriate field.

However the board is composed, it is a good idea (and not at all improper or unethical) to ascertain in advance of the interview who the members are and what groups they represent. When you are introduced to them, you will have some idea of their backgrounds and interests, and at least you will not stutter and stammer over their names.

What should be done before the interview?

While knowledge about the board members is useful and takes some of the surprise element out of the interview, there is other preparation which is more substantive. It *is* possible to prepare for an oral interview – in several ways:

1) Keep a copy of your application and review it carefully before the interview

This may be the only document before the oral board, and the starting point of the interview. Know what education and experience you have listed there, and the sequence and dates of all of it. Sometimes the board will ask you to review the highlights of your experience for them; you should not have to hem and haw doing it.

2) Study the class specification and the examination announcement

Usually, the oral board has one or both of these to guide them. The qualities, characteristics or knowledges required by the position sought are stated in these documents. They offer valuable clues as to the nature of the oral interview. For example, if the job involves supervisory responsibilities, the announcement will usually indicate that knowledge of modern supervisory methods and the qualifications of the candidate as a supervisor will be tested. If so, you can expect such questions, frequently in the form of a hypothetical situation which you are expected to solve. NEVER go into an oral without knowledge of the duties and responsibilities of the job you seek.

3) Think through each qualification required

Try to visualize the kind of questions you would ask if you were a board member. How well could you answer them? Try especially to appraise your own knowledge and background in each area, *measured against the job sought*, and identify any areas in which you are weak. Be critical and realistic – do not flatter yourself.

4) Do some general reading in areas in which you feel you may be weak

For example, if the job involves supervision and your past experience has NOT, some general reading in supervisory methods and practices, particularly in the field of human relations, might be useful. Do NOT study agency procedures or detailed manuals. The oral board will be testing your understanding and capacity, not your memory.

5) Get a good night's sleep and watch your general health and mental attitude

You will want a clear head at the interview. Take care of a cold or any other minor ailment, and of course, no hangovers.

What should be done on the day of the interview?

Now comes the day of the interview itself. Give yourself plenty of time to get there. Plan to arrive somewhat ahead of the scheduled time, particularly if your appointment is in the fore part of the day. If a previous candidate fails to appear, the board might be ready for you a bit early. By early afternoon an oral board is almost invariably behind schedule if there are many candidates, and you may have to wait. Take along a book or magazine to read, or your application to review, but leave any extraneous material in the waiting room when you go in for your interview. In any event, relax and compose yourself.

The matter of dress is important. The board is forming impressions about you – from your experience, your manners, your attitude, and your appearance. Give your personal appearance careful attention. Dress your best, but not your flashiest. Choose conservative, appropriate clothing, and be sure it is immaculate. This is a business interview, and your appearance should indicate that you regard it as such. Besides, being well groomed and properly dressed will help boost your confidence.

Sooner or later, someone will call your name and escort you into the interview room. *This is it.* From here on you are on your own. It is too late for any more preparation. But remember, you asked for this opportunity to prove your fitness, and you are here because your request was granted.

What happens when you go in?

The usual sequence of events will be as follows: The clerk (who is often the board stenographer) will introduce you to the chairman of the oral board, who will introduce you to the other members of the board. Acknowledge the introductions before you sit down. Do not be surprised if you find a microphone facing you or a stenotypist sitting by. Oral interviews are usually recorded in the event of an appeal or other review.

Usually the chairman of the board will open the interview by reviewing the highlights of your education and work experience from your application – primarily for the benefit of the other members of the board, as well as to get the material into the record. Do not interrupt or comment unless there is an error or significant misinterpretation; if that is the case, do not hesitate. But do not quibble about insignificant matters. Also, he will usually ask you some question about your education, experience or your present job – partly to get you to start talking and to establish the interviewing "rapport." He may start the actual questioning, or turn it over to one of the other members. Frequently, each member undertakes the questioning on a particular area, one in which he is perhaps most competent, so you can expect each member to participate in the examination. Because time is limited, you may also expect some rather abrupt switches in the direction the questioning takes, so do not be upset by it. Normally, a board member will not pursue a single line of questioning unless he discovers a particular strength or weakness.

After each member has participated, the chairman will usually ask whether any member has any further questions, then will ask you if you have anything you wish to add. Unless you are expecting this question, it may floor you. Worse, it may start you off on an extended, extemporaneous speech. The board is not usually seeking more information. The question is principally to offer you a last opportunity to present further qualifications or to indicate that you have nothing to add. So, if you feel that a significant qualification or characteristic has been overlooked, it is proper to point it out in a sentence or so. Do not compliment the board on the thoroughness of their examination – they have been sketchy, and you know it. If you wish, merely say, "No thank you, I have nothing further to add." This is a point where you can "talk yourself out" of a good impression or fail to present an important bit of information. Remember, *you close the interview yourself*.

The chairman will then say, "That is all, Mr. _____, thank you." Do not be startled; the interview is over, and quicker than you think. Thank him, gather your belongings and take your leave. Save your sigh of relief for the other side of the door.

How to put your best foot forward

Throughout this entire process, you may feel that the board individually and collectively is trying to pierce your defenses, seek out your hidden weaknesses and embarrass and confuse you. Actually, this is not true. They are obliged to make an appraisal of your qualifications for the job you are seeking, and they want to see you in your best light. Remember, they must interview all candidates and a non-cooperative candidate may become a failure in spite of their best efforts to bring out his qualifications. Here are 15 suggestions that will help you:

1) **Be natural – Keep your attitude confident, not cocky**

If you are not confident that you can do the job, do not expect the board to be. Do not apologize for your weaknesses, try to bring out your strong points. The board is interested in a positive, not negative, presentation. Cockiness will antagonize any board member and make him wonder if you are covering up a weakness by a false show of strength.

2) **Get comfortable, but don't lounge or sprawl**

Sit erectly but not stiffly. A careless posture may lead the board to conclude that you are careless in other things, or at least that you are not impressed by the importance of the occasion. Either conclusion is natural, even if incorrect. Do not fuss with your clothing, a pencil or an ashtray. Your hands may occasionally be useful to emphasize a point; do not let them become a point of distraction.

3) **Do not wisecrack or make small talk**

This is a serious situation, and your attitude should show that you consider it as such. Further, the time of the board is limited – they do not want to waste it, and neither should you.

4) Do not exaggerate your experience or abilities
In the first place, from information in the application or other interviews and sources, the board may know more about you than you think. Secondly, you probably will not get away with it. An experienced board is rather adept at spotting such a situation, so do not take the chance.

5) If you know a board member, do not make a point of it, yet do not hide it
Certainly you are not fooling him, and probably not the other members of the board. Do not try to take advantage of your acquaintanceship – it will probably do you little good.

6) Do not dominate the interview
Let the board do that. They will give you the clues – do not assume that you have to do all the talking. Realize that the board has a number of questions to ask you, and do not try to take up all the interview time by showing off your extensive knowledge of the answer to the first one.

7) Be attentive
You only have 20 minutes or so, and you should keep your attention at its sharpest throughout. When a member is addressing a problem or question to you, give him your undivided attention. Address your reply principally to him, but do not exclude the other board members.

8) Do not interrupt
A board member may be stating a problem for you to analyze. He will ask you a question when the time comes. Let him state the problem, and wait for the question.

9) Make sure you understand the question
Do not try to answer until you are sure what the question is. If it is not clear, restate it in your own words or ask the board member to clarify it for you. However, do not haggle about minor elements.

10) Reply promptly but not hastily
A common entry on oral board rating sheets is "candidate responded readily," or "candidate hesitated in replies." Respond as promptly and quickly as you can, but do not jump to a hasty, ill-considered answer.

11) Do not be peremptory in your answers
A brief answer is proper – but do not fire your answer back. That is a losing game from your point of view. The board member can probably ask questions much faster than you can answer them.

12) Do not try to create the answer you think the board member wants
He is interested in what kind of mind you have and how it works – not in playing games. Furthermore, he can usually spot this practice and will actually grade you down on it.

13) Do not switch sides in your reply merely to agree with a board member
Frequently, a member will take a contrary position merely to draw you out and to see if you are willing and able to defend your point of view. Do not start a debate, yet do not surrender a good position. If a position is worth taking, it is worth defending.

14) Do not be afraid to admit an error in judgment if you are shown to be wrong

The board knows that you are forced to reply without any opportunity for careful consideration. Your answer may be demonstrably wrong. If so, admit it and get on with the interview.

15) Do not dwell at length on your present job

The opening question may relate to your present assignment. Answer the question but do not go into an extended discussion. You are being examined for a *new* job, not your present one. As a matter of fact, try to phrase ALL your answers in terms of the job for which you are being examined.

Basis of Rating

Probably you will forget most of these "do's" and "don'ts" when you walk into the oral interview room. Even remembering them all will not ensure you a passing grade. Perhaps you did not have the qualifications in the first place. But remembering them will help you to put your best foot forward, without treading on the toes of the board members.

Rumor and popular opinion to the contrary notwithstanding, an oral board wants you to make the best appearance possible. They know you are under pressure – but they also want to see how you respond to it as a guide to what your reaction would be under the pressures of the job you seek. They will be influenced by the degree of poise you display, the personal traits you show and the manner in which you respond.

ABOUT THIS BOOK

This book contains tests divided into Examination Sections. Go through each test, answering every question in the margin. We have also attached a sample answer sheet at the back of the book that can be removed and used. At the end of each test look at the answer key and check your answers. On the ones you got wrong, look at the right answer choice and learn. Do not fill in the answers first. Do not memorize the questions and answers, but understand the answer and principles involved. On your test, the questions will likely be different from the samples. Questions are changed and new ones added. If you understand these past questions you should have success with any changes that arise. Tests may consist of several types of questions. We have additional books on each subject should more study be advisable or necessary for you. Finally, the more you study, the better prepared you will be. This book is intended to be the last thing you study before you walk into the examination room. Prior study of relevant texts is also recommended. NLC publishes some of these in our Fundamental Series. Knowledge and good sense are important factors in passing your exam. Good luck also helps. So now study this Passbook, absorb the material contained within and take that knowledge into the examination. Then do your best to pass that exam.

EXAMINATION SECTION

EXAMINATION SECTION
TEST 1

DIRECTIONS: Each question or incomplete statement is followed by several suggested answers or completions. Select the one that BEST answers the question or completes the statement. *PRINT THE LETTER OF THE CORRECT ANSWER IN THE SPACE AT THE RIGHT.*

1. Experience with the city fire prevention program generally demonstrates that   1.____

   A. fires have increased in the public areas of ghetto multiple dwellings despite intensive inspections
   B. inspections are ineffective in both loft buildings and ghetto multiple dwellings
   C. the extensive educational program in the schools resulted in decreases in the number of fires and false alarms when the children reached adulthood
   D. fires have increased in the living areas of ghetto multiple dwellings

2. Assume that a number of alarms relating to manhole fires are received following a surprising spring snowfall. Each officer in command at the various locations transmits to the dispatcher a color code message indicating the severity of the condition.   2.____
   The one of the following conditions for which the WRONG color code message has been transmitted is:

   A. A fire has blown several manhole covers and the Fire Department is standing by - Code Red
   B. Smoke is emanating from manholes under pressure and the Fire Department is standing by - Code Orange
   C. A fire where electrical service around a switch (main fuse box) is affected by a fire that originated within a building - Code White
   D. There is leakage from a gas main in the area - Code Red

3. The one of the following automatic fire alarm detectors that works on the principle of uneven expansion of bimetallic strips is the _____ device.   3.____

   A. rate compensation   B. ionization type
   C. rate of rise type   D. fixed temperature

4. A chief officer supervising a company drill in the use of rapid water noted the following four points made in the summary by the company officer: 4.____
   I. Hand lines stretched from a rapid water pumper shall use a minimum of four lengths of 1 3/4" hose
   II. It is permissible to use 2½" hose to fill out hand lines only if a minimum of 4 lengths of 1 3/4" hose is used as lead lengths
   III. While rapid water is being pumped through a hose line, the booster tank should be filled slowly
   IV. At the conclusion of operations in freezing weather, all gate valves shall be drained completely to prevent ice from forming around the flow sensors
   Of the points emphasized by the company officer, the chief officer should correct the company officer on point _____ since points _____ are correct.

   A. I; II, III, and IV   B. II; I, III, and IV
   C. III; I, II, and IV   D. IV; I, II, and III

5. At a fire in an apartment in a non-fireproof multiple dwelling, a chief ordered the officer of the ladder company to hold off on venting the fire escape windows of the apartment until water arrived at the nozzle of the first hose line at the interior door.
The chief's order was

   A. *correct*, primarily because the hose line was ready to prevent the spread of fire
   B. *incorrect*, primarily because venting should precede moving the line into the apartment with enough time for heat and smoke to dissipate
   C. *correct*, primarily because property losses would thereby be minimized
   D. *incorrect*, primarily because venting of the roof bulkhead should precede venting of the apartment windows

6. Conventional (protein) foam is generally considered MOST appropriate for use

   A. on horizontal surfaces where the cooling effect of water is needed
   B. as an extinguishing agent for fire involving liquefied compressed gases
   C. on electrical fires
   D. to extinguish fires in vessels containing high viscosity oils which have been burning for extended periods of time

7. An exterior beam or girder that frames over an opening, such as a window or doorway, is known as a

   A. tie   B. header   C. trimmer   D. spandrel

8. Under firefighting conditions during civil disorders, the one of the following which is the MOST valid statement is that

   A. greater attention should be given to protection of liquor stores because they are prime targets for arsonists
   B. citizens' band radios should be used for high priority communications to relieve fire department radio systems
   C. response to alarms should be made with minimum use of sirens and reduced speed of apparatus
   D. aggressive attack is essential for complete extinguishment

9. While inspecting a location where swimming pool supplies and chemicals are stored, a chief officer notices various practices involving containers marked *Calcium Hypochlorite*. Of the following employee actions, the one which should be brought to the attention of the management of the firm because it is *unsafe* is:

   A. Handling of the chemical while wearing canvas gloves
   B. Using a metal spoon to scoop up the chemical
   C. Diluting the chemical by pouring it into a large container of water and stirring
   D. Washing away small amounts of spilled chemical with large quantities of water

10. Assume that an officer is in command at a fire where the members of Engine Company 1 were exposed to the effects of high heat without masks and the members of Engine Company 2 used masks under heat and heavy exertion conditions. The officer then ordered Engine 1 members to don masks and to return to work in the contaminated area, and Engine 2 members to continue wearing masks in the contaminated area for the finishing-up phases of the fire. This officer's orders were

A. *correct* for Engine 1 but *incorrect* for Engine 2
B. *correct* for Engine 2 but *incorrect* for Engine 1
C. *correct* for both companies
D. *incorrect* for both companies

11. At a neighborhood community organization meeting and discussion on *Fire Safety In The Home,* a woman asked the officer representing the Fire Department where spot-type heat detectors should be placed in a room to give an alarm properly if fire should occur. The officer responded that the center of the ceiling was the best location. He added that any point on the ceiling was the next best, and, if it were necessary to mount the detector on a side wall, it should be placed at least 6 inches but no more than 12 inches from the ceiling. The officer's instructions to the citizen were   11.____

   A. *correct*
   B. *incorrect* in his statement of *any point on the ceiling;* spot-type detectors should not be placed on ceilings in the corner of rooms
   C. *incorrect* in his statement *at least 6 inches from the ceiling*
   D. *incorrect;* side wall locations for spot-type detectors are preferable to ceiling locations

12. When fighting fires in brownstone dwellings, the LEAST priority should be given to   12.____

   A. build-up of heat and smoke on the top floor
   B. single open interior stairs becoming involved in fire
   C. extension of fire to exposed buildings
   D. poor integrity of rooms, voids in construction, hot air ducts and registers permitting interior fire extension

13. The one of the following which is generally the RECOMMENDED action to take when fighting a fire in finely divided bulk sulphur is to   13.____

   A. use solid streams under pressure, sweeping flames away from uninvolved areas
   B. direct CO_2 extinguishers at the base of the pile so that vapors are carried to the top of the pile by heat waves
   C. apply water sprays so that they settle on the sulphur without disturbing it
   D. dig out the sulphur, examine it, and extinguish the fire by shoveling the sulphur into water pools

14. The shut sprinkler control valve is one of industry's greatest fire hazards. When it is necessary to shut down a system for repairs or other reasons, certain precautions should be taken.
Of the following statements regarding such precautions, the LEAST acceptable is to   14.____

   A. have the system shut down during non-working hours
   B. have the system shut down during working hours while normal operations are going on
   C. notify the Fire Department of the intended shutdown
   D. prepare to supply the system through the two-inch drain in event of an emergency or fire

15. Recognition of shock in a victim and administration of proper first aid measures may be the means of saving life. The one of the following which is the MOST complete and accurate description of the shock condition is:

    A. Pale and cool skin later becoming bluish, lackluster look of the eyes, veins of the hands barely visible
    B. Pale and cool skin later becoming bluish, lackluster look of the eyes, veins of the hands bulging and readily visible
    C. Pink skin, warm perspiration about the head, veins of the hand barely visible
    D. Pink skin, warm perspiration about the head, veins of the hand bulging and readily visible

16. Realistic fire tests to determine the actual burning characteristics of several rigid foam plastic wall and roof assemblies have been conducted within recent years. Of the following conclusions, the one BEST supported by this research is that

    A. low flame spread, rigid polystyrene foam, encased in aluminum skins, required automatic sprinkler protection for satisfactory performance under fire conditions
    B. low flame spread, rigid polyurethane foam, encased in aluminum skins, required automatic sprinkler protection for satisfactory performance under fire conditions
    C. rigid, foamed polyurethane products produce minimum fire contribution when sprayed on walls
    D. materials with a small-scale flame spread rating of 25 are practically self-extinguishing

17. MAXIMUM effectiveness of fireboats in controlling oil spills on water with a fireboat monitor stream is achieved by using the

    A. largest solid stream tip available, with the monitor at horizontal elevation and the stream directed toward the same spot for several minutes
    B. smallest solid stream tip available, with the monitor at horizontal elevation and the stream directed at the same spot for several minutes
    C. largest solid stream tip available, with the monitor at an elevation of 15° above the horizontal
    D. smallest solid stream tip available, with the monitor at an elevation of 15° above the horizontal

18. A chief officer arrives at the scene of an alarm to find that the lieutenant in command of the first arriving ladder company has made no effort to effect forcible entry. The lieutenant explains that the structure is a bonded warehouse with locks sealed by the Federal Government.
    An odor of smoke is coming from the building.
    Of the following, the MOST appropriate *initial* action for the chief to take is to

    A. ask the dispatcher to obtain authorization from the United States Treasury Department to enter the premises
    B. order the door locks broken and entry to be made in order to undertake appropriate operational steps
    C. have ladders raised and entry effected through windows so as to avoid destroying the government seals
    D. request by radio from the borough chief on duty permission to enter the premises by whatever means necessary

19. Extensive loss of blood can be a threat to a person's survival. To control severe bleeding, a tourniquet is sometimes used.
    Of the following statements regarding the use of a tourniquet, the LEAST appropriate is that the

    A. use of a tourniquet may be considered when all other methods have failed
    B. decision to apply a tourniquet is really a decision to risk sacrificing a limb in order to save a life
    C. tourniquet should be loosened every half hour until the arrival of a physician or qualified medical personnel
    D. tourniquet should be placed immediately above the joint if the wound is in a joint area

19.____

20. A 30% increase in false alarms was recorded recently in the city. There was no obvious explanation for this increase.
    The one of the following which is the LEAST acceptable statement with regard to this false alarm problem is that the

    A. increase was recorded principally in certain parts of the city
    B. increase would have been greater but for the introduction of the emergency response system
    C. Fire Department educational program was to be extended by involving local school boards
    D. newly installed push-button street call boxes seemed to attract youths to try them out

20.____

21. The one of the following which is NOT generally considered to be an example of an unsafe act is

    A. operating a line on an icy roof without being secured by a rope around the waist tied to a substantial object
    B. failure to use hose tags
    C. a member positioning himself so that a hoseline is between himself and the edge of the roof
    D. members getting between pumper and edge of pier while apparatus is moving in preparation for drafting water

21.____

22. A chief in command at a fire in a wholesale baking plant orders the low pressure gas supply to the plant shut off. The SAFEST and MOST effective procedure for carrying out this order is to shut off the gas meter valve, shut off the main service valve,

    A. shut off the curb valve, and shut off the street valve
    B. check for the presence of a curb valve and, if present, shut it off
    C. and shut off the street valve
    D. and ignore the curb and street valves

22.____

23. Comnunity relations and fire prevention education efforts must be concentrated in residential neighborhoods, particularly in the depressed areas of the city.
The one of the following which does NOT provide support for this point of view is that

    A. residential occupants are exposed to more serious occupancy hazards than industrial workers
    B. open hydrants, excessive false alarms, and hostile acts are concentrated in depressed areas
    C. rubbish fires and vacant building fires are most frequent in these areas
    D. the primary incidence of fire takes place in residential areas

24. *Limberboards* is a term used to describe the

    A. passages leading to aircraft wing tanks
    B. wood beams covering third rails in the subway system
    C. portable floor covering used to convert hockey rinks for basketball games
    D. wood coverings that protect ships' bilges

25. It is common to find self-closing doors kept open with wooden wedges or other fastenings. To eliminate such unsafe hazards, hooks, fitted wire fusible links, have been designed to hold the doors open.
Generally, these hooks are

    A. *desirable,* if placed low enough for convenient use
    B. *undesirable,* unless placed behind doors, where they would not be subject to damage
    C. *desirable,* if used only on stair and corridor doors
    D. *undesirable* under practically all conditions

KEY (CORRECT ANSWERS)

1.	D	11.	B
2.	A	12.	C
3.	D	13.	C
4.	C	14.	B
5.	A	15.	A
6.	A	16.	A
7.	D	17.	A
8.	C	18.	B
9.	A	19.	C
10.	B	20.	B

21. C
22. B
23. A
24. D
25. D

TEST 2

DIRECTIONS: Each question or incomplete statement is followed by several suggested answers or completions. Select the one that BEST answers the question or completes the statement. *PRINT THE LETTER OF THE CORRECT ANSWER IN THE SPACE AT THE RIGHT.*

1. On visiting a ladder company's quarters, an officer notices a rather *old-looking* manila roof rope.
   The one of the following which is the BEST method for the officer to use in verifying the age of the rope is to

   A. work the strands loose to see how much disintegration has occurred
   B. cut through the strands near the end of the rope in order to find the date marker
   C. examine closely the entire length of the rope while the firemen maintain a pull test on it
   D. call the division of repairs and transportation to check the issue date

2. Some communities have a program for inspecting dwellings, conducted as a courtesy and service to householders.
   The *usual* effect of a dwelling-house inspection campaign is

   A. annoyance on the part of homeowners and their refusal to admit firemen
   B. anticipation of firemen's visits by cleaning up before their arrival
   C. avoidance of major problems found by firemen and their stressing instead the easily corrected conditions
   D. embarrassment of both firemen and homeowners by the procedure and their seeking premature termination of the visit

3. Of the following agents for transferring flammable and combustible liquids, the BEST one is

   A. air pressure
   B. hydraulic or inert gas
   C. straight gravity discharge systems
   D. positive displacement pumps

4. The PRIMARY function of the battalion chief communications coordinator at a third-alarm fire is to

   A. monitor the tactical channel to insure that emergency transmissions are received and acknowledged by the officer in command
   B. call units at the scene to see that their handie-talkies are operating and that their location is properly charted on the command control chart
   C. set up a secondary tactical channel for use by part of the operating units
   D. investigate immediately the reason for failure of contact with an operating unit

5. When relaying water to supply a tower ladder stang intelligent nozzle stream, the pumper closest to the tower ladder should be a recent model pumper.
   This is REQUIRED because

   A. of the greater capacity of these pumpers
   B. of the greater assurance of performance
   C. these pumpers operate at the needed pressures
   D. their gated inlets and relief valves are essential

6. Water must NOT be used under any circumstances to extinguish fires involving the metal

   A. titanium B. zirconium C. magnesium D. calcium

7. The one of the following which is the *generally* recommended procedure when fighting a fire in a racked storage warehouse which has both ceiling and in-rack sprinklers is:

   A. The rack sprinklers should be shut off before the ceiling sprinklers
   B. The ceiling sprinklers should be shut off before the rack sprinklers
   C. All sprinklers should be shut off and hose streams should be applied to the flues between pallet loads
   D. All sprinklers should be shut off as soon as the vents are actuated

8. At a liquefied natural gas spill emergency, a chief finds that the spilled liquid has pooled. To increase the rate of vaporization, he orders that water be applied to the pool as a fine spray. Contact between the LNG and water forms a white solid which has the appearance of slush or snow and floats on the water.
   Of the following, the *recommended* procedure for dealing with this situation is to

   A. let the white solid and pool evaporate under cover of the water spray
   B. use solid streams to break up the white solid in order to expose the liquid below
   C. apply dry chemical to the surface of the white solid to minimize the ignition hazard
   D. shovel the white solid off the pool surface and remove it to a protected area

9. Of the following orders an officer in charge of a serious fire occurring during a performance in a legitimate theater might give, the one which would be LEAST appropriate is to

   A. vent the skylight over the stage
   B. open all exit doors immediately, even before hose lines are in place
   C. reduce pressures in hose lines to allow for ease of movement through the excited audience
   D. raise ladders to fire escape balconies

10. The one of the following MOST likely to inhibit arsonists from using public utility piped gas to commit arson is

    A. inability to control the time lag to ignition
    B. premature discovery because of the telltale odor
    C. difficulty of eliminating suspicion about the source of ignition
    D. ease with which the causes and origins of explosions and fires are determined

11. Experience with buildings collapsing after fire or explosion *generally* shows that

    A. a high survival rate is found in residential buildings that collapse in *pancake* fashion
    B. radiant heat released from a collapsed residential building is of minor significance
    C. pilasters make a masonry wall more vulnerable to collapse
    D. masonry walls that are thinner on upper floors than on lower floors are more likely to collapse

12. A chief in charge of a sector of a fire in a building with large open floors notices that several windows are big enough to permit entrance of the tower ladder boom. As the fire extends throughout the floor and a stream from the tower ladder basket would be more effective inside the building, the chief orders the boom placed through a large window with a stream sweeping the floor. The chief's orders are

    A. *incorrect;* better penetration of the stream could be effected from outside the building
    B. *correct;* this is a good aggressive attack on the fire
    C. *incorrect;* he should first have received permission from the officer in command of the fire
    D. *correct;* considerable manpower and water needs can be saved by an inside attack

13. An engine is pumping through 600 feet of inch rubber-lined hose into the Siamese connection of a building standpipe. Two lengths of inch rubber-lined hose with a 1 1/8 inch nozzle stretch from the standpipe outlet on the tenth floor. The nozzle pressure obtained is 45 pounds per square inch.
    A chief officer deems it advisable to supplement the inch line to the siamese connection. He orders an additional line of 600 feet of 3 inch rubber-lined hose stretched from the same pumper, and indicates that the 45 pounds per square inch nozzle pressure is to remain unchanged.
    The reduction in the required engine pressure resulting from the chief's action is MOST NEARLY

    A. 10%   B. 20%   C. 35%   D. 50%

14. While inspecting a cylindrical gravity tank for an automatic sprinkler system, a chief observes that the water in the tank is 10 feet deep and that the tank has a diameter of 9 feet. He asks the building manager how many gallons are in the tank and receives the reply, *About 10,000.*
    Based on his own observation and calculations, the chief should

    A. agree that the manager's answer is probably correct
    B. disagree with the manager's answer; the answer is more nearly 20,000 gallons
    C. disagree with the manager's answer; the answer is more nearly 15,000 gallons
    D. disagree with the manager's answer; the answer is more nearly 5,000 gallons

15. The official manual of fire communications describes the circumstances when and how field headquarters shall be established by the officer in command. Following are three statements concerning such field headquarters that might be correct:
    I. Field headquarters shall be established when all first alarm engine and ladder companies are operating
    II. The vehicle of the battalion chief originally in command, located close to the officer presently in command, shall be used as field headquarters until the incident is reported under control or the field communications unit arrives
    III. The vehicle serving as field headquarters shall display the Mars or dome light; all other units so equipped or displaying any type of flashing red light shall switch off such lights

    Which of the following choices lists all of the above statements that are correct?

    A. I and II, but not III
    B. II and III, but not I
    C. I and III, but not II
    D. I, II, and III

16. According to the directives governing manning policy, the MAXIMUM number of hours that a fireman in between 9x6 tours may be permitted to work overtime on a partial tour is

    A. 3   B. 4   C. 5   D. 6

17. At an outdoor drill, Lieutenant White, Engine Company 99, and Lieutenant Brown, Ladder Company 99, were discussing the value of initiative in improvising at fires and the need for safety in certain key parts of the evolutions. Lieutenant White stated that in the evolution *Stretch Line Via Aerial Ladder,* it is very important for the safety of the nozzleman, No. 1 man up the aerial ladder, to know the specific things to do at the top of the ladder. Lieutenant Brown thought it was more important to get the hose line on the floor regardless of the procedure. At this point, Chief Jones pointed out that the sequence of moves by the nozzleman at the top of the aerial ladder was designed to minimize the danger of his being yanked off the ladder by an accidental pulling back of the hose line. Chief Jones then reviewed the sequence of moves.
    According to official practice, which of the following choices BEST indicates the correct moves?
    Nozzleman (No. 1)

    A. passes the nozzle and hose in over the sill to the officer, snaps the life belt on the top rung of the ladder, and lightens up on the hose line
    B. moves up with the nozzle and hose over the top rung of the ladder in on the floor
    C. snaps the life belt on the top rung of the ladder and passes the nozzle and hose in over the sill to the officer
    D. snaps his life belt on the top rung of the ladder and places the nozzle and hose over the sill; No. 2 man snaps his life belt on the second rung from the top of the ladder; nozzleman (No. 1) unsnaps his life belt, climbs in the window, and assists the No. 2 man in pulling up sufficient hose

18. The corresponding code letters to be used in the flagging column to locate entries concerning supplies received are

    A. Sup   B. SR   C. P   D. PR

19. When police coverage has not been provided as required at locations where missile throwing and harassment were particularly acute, upon return to quarters, the battalion chief should report the facts to the

    A. police department
    B. office of the chief of department
    C. deputy chief of his division
    D. deputy chief in charge of the fire district

20. Following are three purposes that might be served by written fire and emergency reports:
    I. To prove fire and emergency losses to organizations such as insurance companies and the Internal Revenue Service
    II. To determine the number of deaths and severity of injuries suffered by civilians and department personnel
    III. To affect many major policy decisions made by the department

    Which of the following choices indicates those of the above that are the MAIN purposes of written fire and emergency reports?

    A. I and II, but not III   B. II and III, but not I
    C. I and III, but not II   D. I, II, and III

21. The apparatus inventory list shall be examined for completeness and signed by 21._____

    A. the battalion chief on duty when the list is completed
    B. the battalion chief in the battalion where the apparatus is sent for use
    C. a battalion chief in the battalion where the apparatus is stored
    D. a deputy chief in the division where the apparatus is stored

22. A member initiates a grievance at step I on a grievable matter. The hearing officer lacks 22._____
    authority to grant the solution desired by the grievant.
    The one of the following which is NOT an appropriate procedure for the hearing officer to follow in these circumstances is to

    A. let the aggrieved member or his representative discuss the claim
    B. give a decision appropriate to his authority
    C. discuss the merits of the issue
    D. dismiss the grievance and terminate the proceedings

23. A captain receives an order from a deputy chief which he considers unfair. He explains 23._____
    his problem verbally to his battalion chief. The battalion chief speaks to the deputy chief concerned, who modifies the order to the satisfaction of the captain.
    This action by the battalion chief is

    A. *proper,* mainly because such issues should be settled informally
    B. *improper,* mainly because such action undermines the authority of the deputy chief
    C. *proper,* mainly because it permits the deputy chief to *save face*
    D. *improper,* mainly because he should advise the captain to file a formal grievance in writing

24. Depending on time and circumstances, when an apparatus is placed out of service, it is 24._____
    required that company members be detailed to units within the battalion. Such details should be made by the

    A. administrative battalion chief
    B. battalion commander
    C. administrative deputy chief
    D. officer on duty, after consulting with the battalion chief

25. Battalion chiefs receiving *Lost Property* forms from units reporting losses occurring at a 25._____
    fire shall

    A. cause an immediate investigation to be instituted
    B. personally investigate and record results in endorsement
    C. indicate on the forms results of investigative action taken
    D. attach the findings of the fire marshal assigned and endorse and forward the forms promptly

KEY (CORRECT ANSWERS)

1.	B	11.	A
2.	B	12.	C
3.	D	13.	C
4.	A	14.	D
5.	D	15.	D
6.	D	16.	D
7.	B	17.	C
8.	A	18.	D
9.	C	19.	B
10.	B	20.	C

21. D
22. D
23. A
24. A
25. C

TEST 3

DIRECTIONS: Each question or incomplete statement is followed by several suggested answers or completions. Select the one that BEST answers the question or completes the statement. *PRINT THE LETTER OF THE CORRECT ANSWER IN THE SPACE AT THE RIGHT.*

1. The one of the following which is the MOST valid statement in the fire prevention code regarding height restrictions on combustible fiber storage is that

    A. a clearance of at least 18 inches shall be maintained below the sprinkler head
    B. storage shall be no higher than 20 feet above the floor
    C. storage shall be no higher than 2/3 of the distance from floor to ceiling
    D. storage shall be piled to a height not greater than 6 inches below the top of the enclosing wall

    1.____

2. The one of the following which is NOT among the fire prevention code protection requirements for the storage of television special effects is that

    A. partitions in the storage room shall have at least a one-hour fire resistive rating
    B. the roof of the storage room shall have at least a hour fire resistive rating
    C. there shall be one sprinkler head for each 80 square feet of floor space in the storage room
    D. there shall be mechanical ventilation providing at least four air changes per hour

    2.____

3. According to the fire prevention code, of the following containers, the ones which are NOT legal for the transportation of gasoline are

    A. 5-gallon cans with metal seals
    B. glass bottles not exceeding 4 ounces each
    C. 55-gallon steel barrels or drums
    D. 10-gallon safety cans

    3.____

4. The following conditions have been found during an inspection:
    I. 10,000 small arms cartridges in a store authorized to sell gunpowder
    II. 500 small arms cartridges in a pawnshop
    III. 200 small arms cartridges in a liquor store
    IV. 100 small arms cartridges in a drug store

    Which of the following choices lists ONLY those of the above conditions that comply with the fire prevention code either because a permit may be issued or because a permit is not required?

    A. I, II, and III
    B. I, II, and IV
    C. I, III, and IV
    D. II, III, and IV

    4.____

5. While inspecting a building, an officer notices that a standard enclosure having a three-hour fire resistance rating has been constructed above ground on the lowest floor of the building.
    According to the building code, the MAXIMUM size fuel oil storage tank that can be placed in this enclosure is
    one with a capacity of _____ gallons.

    A. 1,100
    B. 2,500
    C. 10,000
    D. 20,000

    5.____

6. The one of the following which is NOT a Class B multiple dwelling is a

   A. hotel
   B. boarding school
   C. club house
   D. hospital

7. When inspecting an industrial plant, an officer discovers a conveyor passing through a fire wall with no fire shutter for the opening.
   The MOST valid of the following statements concerning alternate forms of protection is that

   A. no alternate is acceptable; a shutter having fire resistance equal to the wall fire resistance is required
   B. a sprinkler head located in the opening to provide at least 3 gallons per square foot per minute is acceptable
   C. two sprinkler heads to provide a water curtain for the entire opening is acceptable
   D. four water spray nozzles on each side of the opening controlled by an automatic valve actuated by a heat detector is acceptable

8. A new restaurant in a multiple-story building of Class I construction has a false front on the outside of the building representing an English castle.
   The one of the following which meets the building code requirement for this condition to be legal is that the false front is of

   A. fire retardant treated wood not over 40 feet high
   B. fire retardant treated wood covering less than 2,000 square feet of surface
   C. slow burning plastic, not over 25 feet high, covering not over 1,000 square feet of surface
   D. slow burning plastic, not over 40 feet high, covering less than 5% of the building surface

9. At a recent fire on the third floor of a building, firemen could not open the locked windows nor could they break the plastic glazing.
   For such conditions, the building code requires that

   A. keys to the windows be available in the lobby
   B. one window for each 50 feet of street front be openable from the inside or outside
   C. all plastic glazing be replaced by glass
   D. all locks be removed and replaced with spring latches

10. Showroom spaces located in office buildings over 100 feet high are required to be sprinklered when the

    A. building air conditioning system serves more than the floor in which the equipment is located, and the showroom space exceeds 7,500 square feet in area and is located more than 40 feet above curb level
    B. showroom space is over 1,000 square feet in area
    C. showroom space is over 7,500 square feet in area, is not equipped with an approved smoke detection alarm system, and is served by a one-floor mechanical ventilation system
    D. showroom space exceeds 2,500 square feet in area and is located more than 75 feet above curb level

11. In a building classified as occupancy group E, occupied or arranged to be occupied for an occupant load of more than one hundred persons above or below the street level or more than a total of five hundred persons in the entire building, a building evacuation supervisor performs his training activities under the direction of

    A. the battalion chief on duty
    B. the building fire safety director
    C. the building fire brigade supervisor
    D. someone other than any of the above

11.____

12. The one of the following which BEST identifies where a Class E fire alarm signal system will sound continuously upon operation of a manual station is only on the floor where

    A. actuated
    B. actuated and the floor above
    C. actuated and the next two floors above
    D. actuated, the floor above, and the floor below

12.____

13. The only one of the following occupancies in which portable kerosene space heaters approved by the board of standards and appeals may be used in the event of failure of the central heating unit is in

    A. private dwellings
    B. multiple dwellings
    C. places of public assembly
    D. schools

13.____

14. The one of the following which is NOT a requirement relating to oxygen and acetylene torch operations in a building under demolition is that there be

    A. one fire guard in the area of torch operation equipped with a 2½" hose line
    B. one fire guard for each torch operator and an additional fire guard on the floor or level below
    C. fire guards to make an inspection of the exposed area one half-hour after completion of torch operations
    D. fire guards to make an inspection of the exposed area one hour after completion of torch operations

14.____

15. Upon responding to an alarm of fire in a building, an officer notes that the siamese connections are painted yellow.
    This color coding indicates that

    A. the sprinkler system protects only showrooms located not over 48 feet above the curb line
    B. the standpipe riser is only four inches in size
    C. a floor control valve is provided for the sprinkler system on each floor
    D. the siamese connection supplies a high-expansion foam system

15.____

16. The one of the following which does NOT correctly describe what can happen during manual operation of an elevator with the keyed switch in the *Fireman Service* position is that the

    A. doors will open on all floors but the fire floor
    B. direction of travel can be changed after a floor selection has been made
    C. doors will open only in response to the *Door Open* button in the car
    D. doors can be automatically reclosed while in the process of opening

17. The building code places restrictions on the suspension of new ceilings below existing suspended ceilings in construction group II in order to restrict the travel of fire in hidden spaces.
    The one of the following requirements which BEST describes the nature of this restriction is that the

    A. concealed space shall be provided with firestops to divide the space into sections not exceeding 3,000 square feet each
    B. new ceiling shall be supported directly from the ceiling carrying channels and shall have no openings from the concealed space to the area below
    C. new ceiling shall be of non-combustible construction or have a flame spread rating of 25 or less, and a smoke developed rating of 50 or less
    D. existing ceiling shall be completely removed before the new ceiling is suspended

18. While inspecting a 125-foot-high factory building constructed in 1912 within 20 feet of an adjacent one story fireproof garage 12 feet in height, an officer notices that the fire windows in the factory wall facing the garage are glazed with wireglass only to the fourth floor or 65-foot level. Windows above that level are 60 feet higher vertically than the roof of the garage and are glazed with inch plate glass lights 400 square inches in area.
    The one of the following which is the PROPER conclusion for the officer to draw is that

    A. such windows comply with the State Labor Law
    B. a violation exists since all fire windows in the wall of a factory building facing any building within 30 feet must be glazed with wireglass
    C. a violation exists since the fire windows in all factory buildings erected before 1913 must have wireglass
    D. none of the fire windows in the factory wall need be wireglass if there are no openings in the garage wall facing it

19. An officer submits for review a referral report containing statements about the exterior screened stairway of a factory building he has recently inspected which he considers to be in violation of the State Labor Law.
    Of the officer's observations listed below, the one that is NOT a violation of the State Labor Law is:

    A. No balcony connecting with the stairs at the fourth floor
    B. Door connecting with the balcony at the third floor opens inward
    C. Stair terminates in rear yard not communicating to a street
    D. Access to balcony at second floor via sliding door

20. A five story non-fireproof factory building erected in 1908 has an area on all floors of 900 square feet with two exits remote from each other on all floors, except for the fourth floor which is used entirely as a raw material storeroom. No one is regularly employed on that floor. For security reasons, the fourth floor has only one exit.
It would be CORRECT to say that, according to the State Labor Law,

    A. this arrangement is expressly forbidden, as every floor must have two exits
    B. one exit from the fourth floor would be acceptable provided it is protected by an automatic sprinkler system
    C. the one exit from the fourth floor is acceptable provided it conforms to the criteria for a factory exit
    D. one exit from the fourth floor is acceptable provided the longest distance to the exit from any point on the floor does not exceed 75 feet

20._____

KEY (CORRECT ANSWERS)

1.	C	11.	B
2.	D	12.	B
3.	D	13.	D
4.	C	14.	A
5.	D	15.	C
6.	D	16.	A
7.	D	17.	D
8.	C	18.	A
9.	B	19.	D
10.	A	20.	C

EXAMINATION SECTION
TEST 1

DIRECTIONS: Each question or incomplete statement is followed by several suggested answers or completions. Select the one that BEST answers the question or completes the statement. *PRINT THE LETTER OF THE CORRECT ANSWER IN THE SPACE AT THE RIGHT.*

1. Of the following materials, the one which has the HIGHEST tendency to spontaneous heating is

    A. lanolin
    B. linseed oil
    C. coconut oil
    D. turpentine

2. The one of the following fabrics used in the manufacture of clothing that is MOST flammable is

    A. wool   B. acetate   C. cotton   D. linen

3. Which of the following substances has the LOWEST boiling point?

    A. Turpentine
    B. Benzene
    C. Mineral spirits
    D. Cellosolve

4. Which of the following non-solid fuels has the HIGHEST ignition temperature?

    A. Acetone
    B. Carbon monoxide
    C. Ethylene
    D. Methyl alcohol

5. Assume that the cellar of a building is 100 feet long, 100 feet wide, and 10 feet high. If natural gas were distributed evenly throughout the cellar, and all openings from the cellar are closed, which one of the following volumes of natural gas would create an explosive atmosphere if suddenly released into this cellar?
   _____ cubic feet.

    A. 2,500   B. 7,500   C. 17,500   D. 25,000

6. A lighted cigarette is LEAST likely to start a fire if dropped and left

    A. on a kapok pillow
    B. on cotton bed clothes
    C. in an explosive vapor-air mixture
    D. on dry grass

7. A fire marshal inspecting a number of buildings where explosions are suspected as having been caused by dynamite would find that the scene of the dynamite explosion is MOST likely the one where

    A. a large section of wall has toppled, with its mortar remaining intact
    B. there are fragments of shattered cast iron
    C. a window frame has been pushed out from the wall surface, with some or all of the windows remaining intact
    D. the light bulbs in the building have remained unbroken

8. During apparatus field inspection of a restaurant located in a building erected in 1972, a fireman finds that the filters for the cooking equipment exhaust system are cleaned every three months and the entire system is cleaned once a year.
   This maintenance procedure is

   A. correct
   B. incorrect, because the filters should be discarded at least every three months and the system cleaned at least once a year
   C. incorrect, because the filters should be discarded at least once a year and the system cleaned at least once a year
   D. incorrect, because both the filters and the entire system should be cleaned at least every three months

9. A group home is a facility for the care and maintenance of not less than three nor more than twelve children and is classified by the building code in the same occupancy group as a one-family dwelling.
   This much of the definition of a group home GENERALLY is

   A. correct
   B. incorrect, because a group home may not have less than seven children
   C. incorrect, because a group home is for adults, not children
   D. incorrect, because a group home is classified in the same occupancy group as a rooming house

10. A fifty-foot high, five-story multiple dwelling built in 1974 has a floor area of 7,000 square feet on each floor. It is equipped with a non-automatic dry standpipe system. During apparatus field inspection duty, a member discovers that a control valve on the standpipe is in closed position with no placard indicating that this was the normal position of the valve. Further investigation reveals that there is no one in the building who has a certificate of fitness to maintain the standpipe system. Of the following statements concerning the above situation, the one that is CORRECT is that the situation as described is

    A. legal
    B. illegal, because an individual with a certificate of fitness must be on the premises
    C. illegal, because an automatic system is required
    D. illegal, because the control valve must be in the open position

11. A tank truck with a capacity of 4,400 gallons is delivering #4 fuel oil to a multiple dwelling. According to the specifications for tank trucks, the person in control of the truck and supervising this delivery

    A. does not require a certificate of fitness because the capacity of the tank is less than 5,000 gallons
    B. does not require a certificate of fitness because the tank has light oil
    C. does not require a certificate of fitness because the delivery is being made to a non-commercial occupancy
    D. requires a certificate of fitness because a fire department permit is needed for all tank trucks delivering #4 fuel oil

12. The multiple dwelling law states that sprinkler systems in lodging houses shall have a supervisory and maintenance service satisfactory to the fire department. The fire department requires a valid inspection of the sprinkler control valve AT LEAST once

A. daily
B. semi-weekly
C. weekly
D. monthly

13. Anhydrous ammonia is being used in a duplicating machine located in a school office. There is no one in the school with a certificate of fitness for the storage and use of ammonia or for the servicing of the duplicating machine. In this situation, a certificate of fitness is GENERALLY 13.____

    A. *not* required because the machine is considered office equipment
    B. *not* required unless the quantity of anhydrous ammonia being stored on the premises is more than two 150-lb. cylinders
    C. *not* required because schools, with regular supervised fire drills, are exempt from certain requirements of the fire prevention code
    D. *required* whether or not a permit is needed under the fire prevention code

14. According to the labor law, fire drills are required to be conducted in certain factory buildings. 14.____
    Which of the following statements is CORRECT with respect to such fire drills?

    A. Fire drills are required to be conducted in every factory building in which there are more than 75 persons above or below the street floor.
    B. Fire drills are not required to be conducted in factory buildings less than 100 feet in height.
    C. Fire drills are required to be conducted in every factory building over two stories in height in which more than twenty-five persons are employed above the ground floor unless the sprinkler system and number of occupants of the building are in accordance with the other provisions of the labor law.
    D. The sprinklering of a factory building is not a factor in determining whether or not a building is required to conduct fire drills.

15. An officer tells members during a drill that a red light and a placard should serve to locate the Siamese hose connection of a temporary standpipe system in a building under construction. 15.____
    The officer's instructions are

    A. *correct*, because both the red light and a placard are required
    B. *incorrect*, because only the red light is required
    C. *incorrect*, because only a placard is required
    D. *incorrect*, because neither the red light nor a placard is required

16. During apparatus field inspection duty, a fireman inspecting a 40-story office building occupied by 1,000 people is unable to find a fire safety director or deputy fire safety director in the building. The manager of the building states that the fire safety director is out to lunch, that there is no deputy fire safety director, and that he, the manager, is acting as the fire safety director pending the return of the fire safety director. Because the manager does not have a fire safety director certificate of fitness, the fireman issues a violation to him. 16.____
    The fireman's action in this situation is

A. *correct,* because local law requires a fire safety director with a certificate of fitness in a building this high to be on duty whenever the building is occupied by more than 500 people
B. *incorrect,* because local law permits the fire safety director to be temporarily relieved, for short intervals, by responsible individuals who do not have the required certificate of fitness
C. *correct,* because local law requires a fire safety director with a certificate of fitness to be on duty in a building this high, regardless of the occupancy of the building
D. *incorrect,* because whenever local law is not complied with, a referral report should be forwarded, and no violation issued

17. A commercial vehicle without a fire department permit is transporting 500 pounds of dynamite from a neighboring outside county through the city to another out-of-town county without stopping to make any deliveries enroute. There is no department pumping engine escort. The situation as described is

    A. *legal,* because the shipment contains less than 1,000 pounds of dynamite
    B. *illegal,* because a pumping engine escort is required whenever explosives are transported without a fire department permit through the city
    C. *legal,* even though a fire department permit has not been issued, because the shipment does not contain any blasting caps
    D. *illegal,* because dynamite may not be transported through the city from one out-of-town location to another

18. Of the following exit doors in buildings erected in 1976, the one that does NOT have to swing outward is a(n)

    A. corridor door from a room used for office purposes with an occupancy of 80 persons
    B. corridor door from a lecture room in a school building where the room has an occupancy of 80 persons
    C. exterior street-floor exit door from a space 2,000 square feet in area in a business building, where the space is occupied by fewer than 50 persons and the maximum travel distance to the door is 50 feet
    D. exterior street-floor exit door from a lobby in a hotel, where the lobby will not be occupied by more than 50 persons and the maximum travel distance to the door is 50 feet

19. During apparatus field inspection duty, a fireman inspecting a 90-foot high apartment house erected in 1972 finds that the standpipe hose is missing from every hose rack in the building. Of the following statements concerning this situation, the one that is CORRECT is that

    A. the situation as described may be legal but the fire-man needs additional information to make a final decision
    B. all such buildings, regardless of when erected, must have the standpipe hose racks equipped with hose
    C. all such buildings, if erected under the new building code, must have their standpipe hose racks equipped with hose
    D. the situation as described would be acceptable for an office building but not for an apartment house

20. A permit is required to store empty combustible packing boxes in a building whenever the

   A. boxes occupy more than two thousand cubic feet
   B. storage space is less than 50 feet from the nearest wall of a building occupied as a hospital, school, or theater
   C. boxes are of cardboard or similarly combustible material
   D. building is of non-fireproof construction

21. An inspector, taking some clothing to a dry cleaner in his neighborhood, noticed that inflammable cleaning fluid was stored in a way which created a fire hazard. The fireman called this to the attention of the proprietor, explaining the danger involved.
   This method of handling the situation was

   A. *bad;* the fireman should not have interfered in a matter which was not his responsibility
   B. *good;* the proprietor would probably remove the hazard and be more careful in the future
   C. *bad;* the fireman should have reported the situation to the fire inspector's office without saying anything to the proprietor
   D. *good;* since the fireman was a customer, he should treat the proprietor more leniently than he would treat other violators

22. According to the Building Code, a vertical iron ladder to an escape manhole opening in the sidewalk is required from a cellar room when the room is being used as a

   A. coal storage room   B. restaurant kitchen
   C. boiler room   D. factory

23. In a building of public assembly, the provisions of the Fire Prevention Code prohibit the use of decorations, drapes, or scenery made of combustible material which have not been rendered fireproof.
   Of the following types of occupancies, the one that is exempt from the provisions of this section is a

   A. school   B. hospital   C. church   D. museum

24. As used in the Building Code, a *4-hour fire rating* of a wall means that in a standard fire test of four hours duration, the

   A. wall will not collapse
   B. unexposed side of the wall will not char or smolder
   C. temperature on the unexposed side of the wall will not rise
   D. temperature on the unexposed side of the wall will not rise more than a predetermined amount

25. The prohibition against smoking in retail stores applies

   A. to all stores
   B. only to stores employing more than 25 persons
   C. only to stores accommodating more than 300 persons
   D. only to stores employing more than 25 persons or accommodating more than 300 persons

KEY (CORRECT ANSWERS)

1.	C	11.	D
2.	D	12.	C
3.	B	13.	D
4.	D	14.	C
5.	C	15.	A
6.	C	16.	D
7.	A	17.	B
8.	D	18.	C
9.	B	19.	A
10.	D	20.	A

21. B
22. C
23. C
24. D
25. A

TEST 2

DIRECTIONS: Each question or incomplete statement is followed by several suggested answers or completions. Select the one that BEST answers the question or completes the statement. *PRINT THE LETTER OF THE CORRECT ANSWER IN THE SPACE AT THE RIGHT.*

1. The one of the following which is NOT required by the Code for the protection of openings into public halls in old-law tenements less than four stories high is that every   1.____

    A. door opening into the public hall shall be fireproof, having a fire-resisting rating of at least one hour
    B. door opening into the public hall shall be self-closing
    C. glazed panel in a door opening into a public hall shall be glazed with wire glass
    D. transom opening upon any public hall shall be glazed with wire glass and firmly secured in a closed position

2. Firestopping of the space above a hung ceiling into areas not exceeding 3,000 square feet is REQUIRED when the   2.____

    A. structural members within the concealed space are individually protected with materials having the required fire resistance
    B. concealed space is sprinklered
    C. ceiling contributes to the required fire resistance of the floor or roof assembly
    D. ceiling is not an essential part of the fire-resistive assembly

3. When a deluge sprinkler system is provided around the perimeter of a theater stage, manual operating devices as well as automatic controls are required by the Building Code.
   The MOST complete and accurate statement concerning these manual operating devices is that they should be located   3.____

    A. at the emergency control station
    B. adjacent to one exit from the stage
    C. at the emergency control station and adjacent to one exit from the stage
    D. at the emergency control station, adjacent to one exit from the stage, and at the deluge valve

4. Yellow painted Siamese caps on office buildings will indicate that the Siamese serves ONLY   4.____

    A. the standpipe in pressurized stairs
    B. the sprinklers in sub-basement locations
    C. a combination standpipe and sprinkler system
    D. as a supply line to the fire pump for the upper level standpipe outlets

5. Of the following buildings, the one that MUST have emergency smoke-venting equipment is a   5.____

    A. new office building, 275 feet high, equipped throughout with automatic sprinklers
    B. new office building, 175 feet high, without an air conditioning system

C. new office building, 75 feet high, without sprinklers and with a central air conditioning system serving more than the floor on which the equipment is located
D. one-story building, classified in occupancy group B-1, greater in depth than 100 feet from a frontage space

6. A factory building was erected in 1912 and was occupied continuously as such until 1950 when it became completely vacant. After many years, it was reoccupied with factory occupancies.
This structure

   A. must comply with the State Labor Law affecting factory buildings erected after October 1, 1913
   B. may be reoccupied as a factory building without changing its classification as one erected before October 1, 1913
   C. may be reoccupied as a factory building erected before October 1, 1913 provided an automatic sprinkler system is installed
   D. cannot be reoccupied as a factory unless it is of fireproof construction

6.____

7. A five-story fireproof factory building erected in 1909 has the following occupancies:
   First floor - dress manufacturing
   Second floor - tannery
   Third floor - artificial flower manufacturing
   Fourth floor - machine shop
   Fifth floor - vacant
Under the State Labor Law, an automatic extinguishing system is

   A. *not required* because the building is classed as fireproof
   B. *required* for the artificial flower factory and all floors above
   C. *not required* if the tannery is moved to the fifth floor
   D. *required* throughout

7.____

8. Which one of the following statements does NOT correctly describe the protection requirements for vertical separation of openings?
In buildings classified in occupancy group

   A. E exceeding three stories or 40 feet in height, openings located vertically above one another in exterior walls except in stairway enclosures required to have a fire resistance rating of one hour or more shall be separated by a spandrel wall at least three feet high between the top of one opening and the bottom of the opening immediately above
   B. D exceeding three stories or 40 feet in height, openings located vertically above one another in exterior walls except in stairway enclosures shall have each such opening above the lower one protected against fire by an opening protective
   C. C exceeding three stories or 40 feet in height, openings located vertically above one another in exterior walls except in stairway enclosures shall be protected by a fire canopy of non-combustible materials extending out at least two feet horizontally from the wall and at least as long as the width of the lower opening
   D. B, spandrels and fire canopies shall be constructed to provide at least the fire-resistance rating required for the exterior wall, but in no event less than one hour

8.____

9. It is MOST complete and accurate to state that, according to the Manual of Fire Communications, in the event the officer in command of a fire or emergency operation requires additional manpower, in lieu of transmitting additional alarms or special calls, he may

   A. telephone the Office of the Chief of Department, specifying the kind of aid required and when it should be sent
   B. notify the dispatcher by radio of the assistance required, specifying the number of officers and fire-men, and the location to which they shall report
   C. telephone the dispatcher specifying the assistance required, including the number of officers and fire-men needed, location to which they shall report, and the expected time additional manpower will be released
   D. notify the Office of the Chief of Department, specifying the assistance required, the location to which they shall report, the reason for calling additional manpower, and the amount of time they can be expected to be detained

10. While inspecting a sprinklered building, a fire officer is asked by the building manager for his opinion about painting the wooden water tank on the roof. The manager explains it is his understanding that painting the tank will extend its useful life.
    Of the following, it would probably be MOST appropriate for the fire officer to indicate that

    A. painting the interior of the tank below water level will prolong the life of the tank, but painting the exterior may tend to hide structural defects
    B. painting a wooden tank may be desirable from the standpoint of appearance, but it is of questionable value in increasing the life of the tank
    C. the use of paint is undesirable for any purpose on either the exterior or interior of the tank
    D. the manager should consult a painting contractor to find out what his experience and recommendations are

11. In a large warehouse facility, the GREATEST fire hazard potential will result if rubber automotive tires are stored on the

    A. side in stacked piles   B. tread in racks
    C. side on pallets   D. tread in stacked piles

12. During a fire prevention inspection, a firefighter may find a condition which could be the immediate cause of death in the event of a fire.
    Which one of the following conditions in a restaurant is the MOST dangerous?

    A. Blocked exit doors
    B. A crack in the front door
    C. A window that does not open
    D. A broken air conditioning system

13. Firefighters must regularly inspect office buildings to determine whether fire prevention laws have been obeyed. Some of these fire prevention laws are as follows: DOORS: Doors should be locked as follows:
    I. Doors on the ground floor may be locked on the street side to prevent entry into the stairway.
    II. Doors in office buildings that are less than 100 feet in height may be locked on the stairway side on each floor above the ground floor.
    III. Doors in office buildings that are 100 feet or more in height may be locked on the stairway side except for every fourth floor.

    The doors in an office building which is less than 100 feet in height may be locked on the stairway side

    A. on all floors including the ground floor
    B. on all floors above the ground floor
    C. except for every fourth floor
    D. on all floors above the fourth floor

14. SIGNS: Signs concerning stairways should be posted in the following manner:
    I. A sign shall be posted near the elevator on each floor, stating, *IN CASE OF FIRE, USE STAIRS UNLESS OTHERWISE INSTRUCTED.* The sign shall contain a diagram showing the location of the stairs and the letter identification of the stairs.
    II. Each stairway shall be identified by an alphabetical letter on a sign posted on the hallway side of the stair door.
    III. Signs indicating the floor number shall be attached to the stairway side of each door.
    IV. Signs indicating whether re-entry can be made into the building, and the floors where re-entry can be made, shall be posted on the stairway side of each door.

    Which one of the following CORRECTLY lists the information which should be posted on the stairway side of a door?

    A sign will indicate the
    A. floor number, whether re-entry can be made into the building, and the floors where re-entry can be made
    B. alphabetical letter of the stairway, whether re-entry can be made into the building, and the floors where re-entry can be made
    C. alphabetical letter of the stairway and the floor number
    D. alphabetical letter of the stairway, the floor number, whether re-entry can be made into the building, and the floors where re-entry can be made

15. The Fire Department now uses companies on fire duty, with their apparatus, for fire prevention inspection in commercial buildings.
    The one of the following changes which was MOST important in making this inspection procedure practicable was the

    A. reduction of hours of work of firemen
    B. use of two-way radio equipment
    C. use of enclosed cabs on fire apparatus
    D. increase in property values during the post-war period

16. The MAXIMUM length of unlined linen hose which shall be permitted at any standpipe hose outlet valve is

   A. 50' B. 75' C. 100' D. 125'

17. The State Labor Law requires that fire drills be conducted monthly in factory buildings over two stories in height in which more than 25 persons are employed above the ground floor.
The one of the following statements that is MOST complete and accurate is that the law provides for automatic exemption from this requirement to factory buildings which are

   A. completely sprinklered
   B. completely sprinklered by a system having two adequate sources of water supply
   C. completely sprinklered by a system having two adequate sources of water supply and a maximum number of occupants of any one floor not more than 50 percent above the capacity of the exits required for the same building if unsprinklered
   D. completely sprinklered by a system having two adequate sources of water supply, a maximum number of occupants of any one floor not more than 50 percent above the capacity of the exits required for the same building if unsprinklered and an interior fire alarm system

18. Automatic sprinkler systems installed in the public halls of converted multiple dwellings with a required Siamese are subjected to a hydrostatic pressure test before acceptance. The test pressure for such systems is to be NOT less than

   A. 30 pounds per square inch
   B. 30 pounds per square inch in excess of the normal pressure required for such systems when in service
   C. 200 pounds per square inch
   D. 200 pounds per square inch in excess of the normal pressure required for such systems when in service

19. According to the rules of the Board of Standards and Appeals, when flameproofed materials are subjected to prescribed tests, they shall meet established standards for each of the following properties EXCEPT

   A. flashing   B. duration of flame
   C. duration of glow   D. temperature of flame

20. Each year many children die in fires which they have started while playing with matches. Of the following measures, the one that would be MOST effective in preventing such tragedies is to

   A. warn the children of the dangers involved
   B. punish parents who are found guilty of neglecting their children
   C. keep matches out of the reach of children
   D. use only safety matches

21. Sparks given off by welding torches are a serious fire hazard.
The BEST of the following methods of dealing with this hazard is to conduct welding operations

    A. only in fireproof buildings protected by sprinkler systems
    B. only out-of-doors on a day with little wind blowing
    C. only on materials certified to be non-combustible by recognized testing laboratories
    D. only after loose combustible materials have been cleared from the area and with a man standing by with a hose line

22. A two-story, Class 3, non-fireproof building was originally occupied as a store on the first floor and one apartment on the second floor. Upon inspection, you find that the second floor is now being used for offices. The building is 20' x 50'. There is one stairway made of wood, enclosed with fire-retarded stud partitions, leading directly to the street from the second floor.
The one of the following statements that is MOST complete and accurate is that the situation as described

    A. complies with applicable laws
    B. is illegal because the stair should be of incombustible material
    C. is illegal because there should be two means of egress
    D. is illegal because there should be two means of egress and the stair should be of incombustible material

Questions 23-25.

DIRECTIONS: Questions 23 through 25 are to be answered SOLELY on the basis of the following passage.

Automatic sprinkler systems are installed in many buildings. They extinguish or keep from spreading 96% of all fires in areas they protect. Sprinkler systems are made up of pipes which hang below the ceiling of each protected area and sprinkler heads which are placed along the pipes. The pipes are usually filled with water, and each sprinkler head has a heat sensitive part. When the heat from the fire reaches the sensitive part of the sprinkler head, the head opens and showers water upon the fire in the form of spray. The heads are spaced so that the fire is covered by overlapping showers of water from the open heads.

23. Automatic sprinkler systems are installed in buildings to

    A. prevent the build-up of dangerous gases
    B. eliminate the need for fire insurance
    C. extinguish fires or keep them from spreading
    D. protect 96% of the floor space

24. If more than one sprinkler head opens, the area sprayed will be

    A. flooded with hot water
    B. overlapped by showers of water
    C. subject to less water damage
    D. about 1 foot per sprinkler head

25. A sprinkler head will open and shower water when 25.____
    A. it is reached by heat from a fire
    B. water pressure in the pipes gets too high
    C. it is reached by sounds from a fire alarm
    D. water temperature in the pipes gets too low

KEY (CORRECT ANSWERS)

1.	A	11.	B
2.	C	12.	A
3.	C	13.	B
4.	C	14.	A
5.	D	15.	B
6.	B	16.	D
7.	D	17.	C
8.	A	18.	C
9.	B	19.	D
10.	B	20.	C

21.	D
22.	A
23.	C
24.	B
25.	A

TEST 3

DIRECTIONS: Each question or incomplete statement is followed by several suggested answers or completions. Select the one that BEST answers the question or completes the statement. *PRINT THE LETTER OF THE CORRECT ANSWER IN THE SPACE AT THE RIGHT.*

1. The one of the following which is the MOST valid statement in the Fire Prevention Code regarding height restrictions on combustible fiber storage is that   1.____

   A. a clearance of at least 18 inches shall be maintained below the sprinkler head
   B. storage shall be no higher than 20 feet above the floor
   C. storage shall be no higher than 2/3 of the distance from floor to ceiling
   D. storage shall be piled to a height not greater than 6 inches below the top of the enclosing wall

2. The one of the following which is NOT among the Fire Prevention Code protection requirements for the storage of television special effects is that   2.____

   A. partitions in the storage room shall have at least a one-hour fire resistive rating
   B. the roof of the storage room shall have at least a 1 1/2 hour fire resistive rating
   C. there shall be one sprinkler head for each 80 square feet of floor space in the storage room
   D. there shall be mechanical ventilation providing at least four air changes per hour

3. According to the Fire Prevention Code, of the following containers, the ones which are NOT legal for the transportation of gasoline are   3.____

   A. 5-gallon cans with metal seals
   B. glass bottles not exceeding 4 ounces each
   C. 55-gallon steel barrels or drums
   D. 10-gallon safety cans

4. The following conditions have been found during an inspection: 4.____
   I. 10,000 small arms cartridges in a store authorized to sell gunpowder
   II. 500 small arms cartridges in a pawn shop
   III. 200 small arms cartridges in a liquor store
   IV. 100 small arms cartridges in a drug store

   Which of the following choices lists ONLY those of the above conditions that comply with the Fire Prevention Code either because a permit may be issued or because a pernit is not required?

   A. I, II, III   B. I, II, IV
   C. I, III, IV   D. II, III, IV

5. While inspecting a building, an officer notices that a standard enclosure having a three-hour fire resistance rating has been constructed above ground on the lowest floor of the building.   5.____
   According to the Building Code, the MAXIMUM size fuel oil storage tank that can be placed in this enclosure is one with a capacity of _____ gallons.

   A. 1,100   B. 2,500   C. 10,000   D. 20,000

6. The one of the following which is NOT a Class B multiple dwelling is a

   A. hotel
   B. boarding school
   C. clubhouse
   D. hospital

7. When inspecting an industrial plant, an officer discovers a conveyor passing through a fire wall with no fire shutter for the opening.
   The MOST valid of the following statements concerning alternate forms of protection is that

   A. no alternate is acceptable; a shutter having fire resistance equal to the wall fire resistance is required
   B. a sprinkler head located in the opening to provide at least 3 gallons per square foot per minute is acceptable
   C. two sprinkler heads to provide a water curtain for the entire opening is acceptable
   D. four water spray nozzles on each side of the opening controlled by an automatic valve actuated by a heat detector is acceptable

8. A new restaurant in a multiple-story building of Class I construction has a false front on the outside of the building representing an English castle.
   The one of the following which meets the Building Code requirement for this condition to be legal is that the false front is of

   A. fire retardant treated wood not over 40 feet high
   B. fire retardant treated wood covering less than 2,000 square feet of surface
   C. slow burning plastic, not over 25 feet high, covering not over 1,000 square feet of surface
   D. slow burning plastic, not over 40 feet high, covering less than 5% of the building surface

9. At a recent fire on the third floor of a building, firemen could not open the locked windows nor could they break the plastic glazing.
   For such conditions, the Building Code requires that

   A. keys to the windows be available in the lobby
   B. one window for each 50 feet of street front be openable from the inside or outside
   C. all plastic glazing be replaced by glass
   D. all locks be removed and replaced with spring latches

10. Showroom spaces located in office buildings over 100 feet high are required to be sprinklered when the

    A. building air conditioning system serves more than the floor in which the equipment is located, and the showroom space exceeds 7,500 square feet in area and is located more than 40 feet above curb level
    B. showroom space is over 1,000 square feet in area and is located more than 40 feet above curb level
    C. showroom space is over 7,500 square feet in area, is not equipped with an approved smoke detection alarm system, and is served by a one-floor mechanical ventilation system
    D. showroom space exceeds 2,500 square feet in area and is located more than 75 feet above curb level

11. In a building classified as occupancy group E, occupied or arranged to be occupied for an occupant load of more than one hundred persons above or below the street level or more than a total of five hundred persons in the entire building, a building evacuation supervisor performs his training activities under the direction of

    A. the battalion chief on duty
    B. the building fire safety director
    C. the building fire brigade supervisor
    D. someone other than any of the above

12. The one of the following which BEST identifies where a Class E fire alarm signal system will sound continuously upon operation of a manual station is only on the floor where

    A. actuated
    B. actuated and the floor above
    C. actuated and the next two floors above
    D. actuated, the floor above, and the floor below

13. The ONLY one of the following occupancies in which portable kerosene space heaters approved by the Board of Standards and Appeals may be used in the event of failure of the central heating unit is in

    A. private dwellings
    B. multiple dwellings
    C. places of public assembly
    D. schools

14. The one of the following which is NOT a requirement relating to oxygen and acetylene torch operations in a building under demolition is that there be

    A. one fire guard in the area of torch operation equipped with a 2 1/2" hose line
    B. one fire guard for each torch operator and an addi-tional fire guard on the floor or level below
    C. fire guards to make an inspection of the exposed area one half hour after completion of torch operations
    D. fire guards to make an inspection of the exposed area one hour after completion of torch operations

15. Upon responding to an alarm of fire in a building, an officer notes that the Siamese connections are painted yellow.
    This color coding indicates that

    A. the sprinkler system protects only showrooms located not over 40 feet above the curb line
    B. the standpipe riser is only four inches in size
    C. a floor control valve is provided for the sprinkler system on each floor
    D. the Siamese connection supplies a high-expansion foam system

16. The one of the following which does NOT correctly describe what can happen during manual operation of an elevator with the keyed switch in the *Fireman Service* position is that the

    A. doors will open on all floors but the fire floor
    B. direction of travel can be changed after a floor selection has been made

C. doors will open only in response to the *Door Open* button in the car
D. doors can be automatically reclosed while in the process of opening

17. The Building Code places restrictions on the suspension of new ceilings below existing suspended ceilings in construction group II in order to restrict the travel of fire in hidden spaces.
The one of the following requirements which BEST describes the nature of this restriction is that the

   A. concealed space shall be provided with firestops to divide the space into sections not exceeding 3,000 square feet each
   B. new ceiling shall be supported directly from the ceiling carrying channels and shall have no openings from the concealed space to the area below
   C. new ceiling shall be of non-combustible construction or have a flame spread rating of 25 or less, and a smoke developed rating of 50 or less
   D. existing ceiling shall be completely removed before the new ceiling is suspended

18. While inspecting a 125-foot-high factory building constructed in 1912 within 20 feet of an adjacent one-story fireproof garage 12 feet in height, an officer notices that the fire windows in the factory wall facing the garage are glazed with wireglass only to the fourth floor or 65-foot level. Windows above that level are 60 feet higher vertically than the roof of the garage and are glazed with inch plate glass lights 400 square inches in area.
The one of the following which is the PROPER conclusion for the officer to draw is that

   A. such windows comply with the State Labor Law
   B. a violation exists since all fire windows in the wall of a factory building facing any building within 30 feet must be glazed with wireglass
   C. a violation exists since the fire windows in all factory buildings erected before 1913 must have wireglass
   D. none of the fire windows in the factory wall need be wireglass if there are no openings in the garage wall facing it

19. An officer submits for review a referral report containing statements about the exterior screened stairway of a factory building he has recently inspected which he considers to be in violation of the State Labor Law.
Of the officer's observations listed below, the one that is NOT a violation of the State Labor Law is:

   A. No balcony connecting with the stairs at the fourth floor
   B. Door connecting with the balcony at the third floor opens inward
   C. Stair terminates in rear yard not communicating to a street
   D. Access to balcony at second floor via sliding door

20. A five story non-fireproof factory building erected in 1908 has an area on all floors of 900 square feet with two exits remote from each other on all floors, except for the fourth floor which is used entirely as a raw material storeroom. No one is regularly employed on that floor. For security reasons, the fourth floor has only one exit.
It would be CORRECT to say that, according to the State Labor Law,

   A. this arrangement is expressly forbidden, as every floor must have two exits
   B. one exit from the fourth floor would be acceptable provided it is protected by an automatic sprinkler system

C. the one exit from the fourth floor is acceptable provided it conforms to the criteria for a factory exit
D. one exit from the fourth floor is acceptable provided the longest distance to the exit from any point on the floor does not exceed 75 feet

21. Buildings which have been vacated by order of the fire department are kept under surveillance.
    When such buildings have been boarded up, surveillance may, with approval, be reduced to once each

    A. week
    B. month
    C. quarter-year
    D. half-year

22. Overly detailed fire prevention inspections are to be avoided CHIEFLY because they

    A. unduly interfere with the normal activities of the occupancy, causing public resentment
    B. require excessive time which could be used to better advantage inspecting other occupancies
    C. tend to result in oversight of some fundamental hazards
    D. are beyond the capabilities of many firemen who are not specifically trained in inspectional techniques

23. Requests for sprinkler re-evaluation are accepted by the fire department, and a re-inspection made, if the petitioner states that substantial changes have been made in the sprinkler system.
    The one of the following statements that is MOST accurate and complete is that such re-inspections are made by the division commander

    A. in all instances
    B. except when he has endorsed the original sprinkler order
    C. except when he has endorsed the original sprinkler order or when his workload is excessive
    D. except when he has endorsed the original sprinkler order, his workload is excessive, or the re-evaluation is extremely complex

24. Department regulations require the forwarding of reports to the Fire Commissioner relating to demolition work adjacent to or adjoining company quarters.
    The one of the following statements that is MOST accurate and complete is that such reports should be forwarded when notice of the proposed demolition is

    A. received
    B. received and when the work is completed
    C. received, when the work actually starts, and when the work is completed
    D. received, when the work actually starts, when any interruption of work occurs, and when the work is completed

25. The one of the following statements that is MOST complete and accurate is that when a building inspector issues a Violation Order, the time allowed for compliance

    A. must be the specific number of days indicated on the Standard Form of Orders
    B. may be less than the specific number of days indicated on the Standard Form of Orders

C. may be more than the specific number of days indicated on the Standard Form of Orders
D. may be more or less than the specific number of days indicated on the Standard Form of Orders, depending upon the circumstances

---

KEY (CORRECT ANSWERS)

1. C
2. D
3. D
4. C
5. D

6. D
7. D
8. C
9. B
10. A

11. B
12. B
13. D
14. A
15. C

16. A
17. D
18. A
19. D
20. C

21. C
22. B
23. D
24. A
25. B

TEST 4

DIRECTIONS: Each question or incomplete statement is followed by several suggested answers or completions. Select the one that BEST answers the question or completes the statement. *PRINT THE LETTER OF THE CORRECT ANSWER IN THE SPACE AT THE RIGHT.*

1. Of the following substances, the one that would MOST appropriately be protected with a sprinkler installation is

    A. cellulose acetate
    B. quicklime
    C. magnesium powder
    D. calcium carbide

    1.____

2. Providing clearance around unprotected steel columns in storage occupancies is a practice which is GENERALLY

    A. *desirable,* chiefly because the quantity of combustibles stored is reduced
    B. *undesirable,* chiefly because flue-like conditions will prevail
    C. *desirable,* chiefly because it will allow water from sprinklers to keep the column wet
    D. *undesirable,* chiefly because stock can topple if not supported

    2.____

3. National fire records indicate that over the years restaurant fires have increased in number and in total dollar loss despite technological improvements.
   The large increase in the number of restaurant fires is PRIMARILY attributable to

    A. fires of incendiary origin
    B. duct fires
    C. the use of open flames for cooking
    D. careless handling of smoking materials

    3.____

4. When serving a summons for a violation of the Building Code, it is most important that proper procedure be followed.
   Of the following statements, the one that is MOST acceptable is that a summons may be

    A. mailed to the residence of the building's owner if he is not on the premises
    B. given to a superintendent to be forwarded to the owner if he is not on the premises
    C. placed on the desk or in the immediate vicinity of the owner if he refuses to accept it
    D. made out with the initials of the owner if the full name is not known

    4.____

5. A dry-pipe sprinkler system is generally not considered acceptable protection for an occupancy utilizing flammable liquids MAINLY because

    A. corrosion tends to weaken these systems
    B. water is a poor extinguishing agent for flammable liquids
    C. the systems are too expensive for the purpose
    D. a fast spreading fire may be out of control by the time water arrives

    5.____

6. In order to enforce the fire safety laws, firefighters must inspect buildings and stores.
   It is NOT a good idea for firefighters to let owners of buildings and stores know when they are coming because

    6.____

A. firefighters will waste valuable time if the owner breaks the appointment
B. owners might try to hide fire hazards from the fire-fighters
C. firefighters can make the inspection faster without an appointment
D. owners would be angry if the firefighters were unable to keep the appointment

7. Many older buildings are modernized to give a blank wall appearance by being *wrapped*. It is INACCURATE to state, with reference to *wrapped* buildings, that

   A. the use of expanded metal panels reduces the hazard from exposure fires
   B. they are essentially windowless buildings
   C. solid metal panels may be blown loose and scale a considerable distance
   D. expanded metal panels may be hung or mounted a foot or more from the original exterior wall

8. According to the Administrative Code, it is unlawful to manufacture within the city all of the following EXCEPT

   A. blank cartridges
   B. railroad track torpedoes
   C. flashlight compositions
   D. ship signal rockets

9. A newly appointed firefighter is assigned to go with an experienced firefighter to inspect a paint store. The paint store owner refuses to allow the inspection, saying that he is closing the store early that day and going on vacation. The new firefighter demands rudely that the inspection be allowed, even though it would be permissible to delay it.
   Of the following, it would be BEST for the experienced firefighter to

   A. repeat the demand that the inspection be allowed and quote the law to the store owner
   B. tell the new firefighter that it would be best to schedule the inspection after the store owner's vacation
   C. tell the store owner to step aside, and instruct the new firefighter to enter the store and begin the inspection
   D. tell the new firefighter to forget about the inspection because the store owner is uncooperative

10. One person shall be permitted to supervise more than one interior fire alarm system. The one of the following that is NOT in accord with the restrictions placed on this permission is that

    A. the buildings in which the interior fire alarm systems are located must be within an area whose diameter does not exceed six hundred feet
    B. the interior fire alarms in all buildings in the group can be tested within thirty minutes of commencing work daily
    C. the addresses of all buildings shall be listed on the one certificate of fitness
    D. records and logbooks must be kept on each premises

11. The one of the following which is NOT in accord with the Regulations for Use of Halon 1301, Extinguishing Agent, is that

    A. maximum concentration shall not exceed 10 percent where human habitation is present in the volume to be flooded
    B. minimum concentration of FE 1301 used shall not be less than 10 percent

C. a discharge rate which results in attaining the design concentration in 8 seconds is acceptable
D. a central office connection must be provided for fire detection or systems operation where human habitation is present in the volume to be flooded

12. According to the Fire Prevention Code, a person who holds a permit for the manufacture of inflammable mixtures and who wishes to manufacture combustible mixtures is

   A. *required* to obtain another permit
   B. *not required* to obtain another permit
   C. *not required* to obtain another permit unless the mixtures include stove polishes or insecticides
   D. *not required* to obtain another permit unless the mixtures include medicinal and toilet preparations

13. The one of the following statements which is MOST accurate and complete is that the Fire Prevention Code permits the hanging of fresh-cut decorative greens in places of public assembly only if they do not contain

   A. pitch
   B. pitch and are hung by means of non-combustible material
   C. pitch, are hung by means of non-combustible material, and do not remain for a period in excess of 24 hours
   D. pitch, are hung by means of non-combustible material, have been treated with an approved evaporation-retarding product, and do not remain for a period in excess of 48 hours

14. In any automatic wet-pipe sprinkler system which has standard one-half inch sprinkler heads exposed to cold and subject to freezing, shut-off valves may be provided and the water supply discontinued

   A. under no circumstances
   B. from November 15 to March 15 when there are five or less such exposed heads
   C. from November 1 to April 1 when there are ten or less such exposed heads
   D. from November 15 to April 15 when there are fifteen or less such exposed heads

15. At an inspection of a building, one floor of which is used for combustible fiber storage, the following facts are revealed:
   I. The safe bearing capacity of the floor, as certified by the Department of Buildings, is 250 lbs./sq.ft. The weight of the combustible fiber is 75 lbs./sq.ft.
   II. The floor is 10,000 sq.ft. in area, of which 6,000 sq.ft. is occupied by the fiber bales.
   III. The height from floor to ceiling is 16', and the stacked bales stand 10' high.
   In this situation, _____ of the Fire Prevention Code.

   A. Item I is in   B. Item II is in
   C. Item III is in   D. there is no

16. Carelessness in smoking is a very common cause of fire.
    A lighted cigarette placed on top of most upholstery will GENERALLY

   A. cause no damage
   B. burn to the end without starting a fire

C. cause a gradually increasing fire
D. start a fire rapidly

17. The one of the following that is the type of automatic sprinkler system MOST commonly found in museums, art galleries, and storage places for records or valuable merchandise is the _____ system.

    A. deluge
    B. pre-action
    C. dry pipe
    D. sypho-chemical

18. The Fire Prevention Code requires that a permit be obtained for the storage of more than the equivalent of five barrels of oils and fats.
    The one of the following which is excluded from this requirement is

    A. lubricating oils
    B. grease
    C. edible oils
    D. soap stock

19. The Fire Prevention Code requires that rooms in dry cleaning establishments in which washing tanks are located be equipped with

    A. asbestos cloths or blankets
    B. carbon dioxide or dry chemical extinguishers
    C. buckets of sand
    D. automatic fire alarm device

20. The one of the following occupancies which is required to have a two-source water supply for its sprinkler system is one containing

    A. combustible fiber storage
    B. a motion picture film studio
    C. oils and fats storage
    D. a theater

21. The one of the following statements that is MOST accurate is that the Fire Prevention Code prohibits the storage of distilled liquors and alcohols in

    A. quantities aggregating more than 50 gallons, without a permit
    B. any building of wooden construction
    C. excess of one barrel for each five square feet of floor space
    D. barrels stacked more than one high

22. A special permit issued by the Fire Commissioner is required for the operation of certain businesses. Concerning parking lots, technical establishments, retail drug stores, and dry cleaning establishments, it is MOST accurate to say that special permits are required for all

    A. four of them
    B. of the above except parking lots
    C. of the above except technical establishments
    D. of the above except retail drug stores

23. The one of the following chemicals which may NOT be manufactured or stored in a drug and chemical supply house in any quantity is

   A. acetone
   B. benzole
   C. chloride of nitrogen
   D. metallic magnesium

24. A permit is required for the storage of empty wooden packing boxes in buildings if the quantity stored exceeds

   A. one ton
   B. 2,000 square feet of area
   C. 2,000 cubic feet of space
   D. one ton or 2,000 square feet of area, whichever is the smaller amount

25. The MAXIMUM number of excess liquefied petroleum gas cylinders that may be stored in a single structure protected by an approved dry sprinkler system is

   A. 25   B. 50   C. 75   D. 100

KEY (CORRECT ANSWERS)

1. A
2. C
3. A
4. C
5. D

6. B
7. A
8. D
9. B
10. C

11. B
12. B
13. C
14. C
15. D

16. B
17. B
18. C
19. A
20. B

21. B
22. A
23. C
24. C
25. B

EXAMINATION SECTION
TEST 1

DIRECTIONS: Each question or incomplete statement is followed by several suggested answers or completions. Select the one that BEST answers the question or completes the statement. *PRINT THE LETTER OF THE CORRECT ANSWER IN THE SPACE AT THE RIGHT.*

1. Assume that you are making an inspection at a plastics manufacturing factory. The plant manager discusses fire safety procedures with you and tells you that he will be having small-scale bench tests made in order to measure various properties of plastics exposed to fire. The manager tells you he expects to gain certain information from these tests. Of the following, you would be correct in telling him that these tests will be MOST effective in evaluating the

   A. tendency of the plastic to melt and drip
   B. relative combustibility of plastics
   C. composition of products of combustion
   D. methods of installation of plastic parts

1.____

2. Assume that your division commander has asked you to prepare a report on minimizing the hazard of dust explosions. This is one in a series of reports to be used to guide industrial plant managers in your division on fire safety precautions.
Of the following, it would be MOST appropriate for you to point out that generally

   A. a high level of moisture in the air will be effective in raising the ignition temperature of most dusts and reducing the deflagration once ignition has occurred
   B. relatively small amounts of inert solid powder will be effective in preventing explosions by reducing the combustibility of a dust through heat absorption
   C. removal of high-temperature sources of ignition will be effective in reducing the possibility of explosion because common ignition sources generally do not provide ignition temperatures required for dust explosions
   D. inert gas will be effective in preventing explosions because it dilutes the oxygen to a concentration too low to support combustion

2.____

3. The selection of smoke removal and venting procedures in hi-rise buildings depends to a large extent on the factors which affect smoke movement in these structures, such as the *stack effect.*
Which one of the following statements about the stack effect is MOST NEARLY correct?

   A. When the outside temperature is much lower than the inside temperature and a fire occurs some distance below the neutral pressure plane, the stack effect will not overcome the fire pressure.
   B. The stack effect will cause smoke and toxic gases to flow through stairwells and elevator shafts, except when the doors of these shafts remain closed.
   C. When the outside temperature is greater than the inside temperature, a reverse stack effect occurs with the upper building opening becoming the inlet and the lower opening the outlet.
   D. The magnitude of the stack effect is a function of building height, air leakage between floors, and the differences between inside and outside temperatures, but is not affected by the air leakage through exterior walls.

3.____

4. Warehouse fires often present a severe challenge to firefighters. A fire officer inspecting a storage warehouse should be aware of proper indoor storage practices and the use of racks and pallets in such storage.
Which one of the following statements regarding storage practices in warehouses is generally CORRECT?

    A. The arrangement of commodities stored in racks generally provides greater flue spaces both horizontally and vertically than palletized general storage.
    B. Storage of empty plastic pallets within warehouses should be in piles limited to eight feet in height.
    C. Stacking idle pallets in piles is unlikely to promote rapid spread of fire, heat release, and complete combustion.
    D. Storage of empty wood pallets in an unsprinklered warehouse containing other storage should be limited to buildings of fireproof construction.

5. The Fire Code provides that, in a dry cleaning establishment, each room where a washing tank is located must be provided with an approved fire extinguishing system.
The type of system which is specified is a(n) _____ system.

    A. steam   B. carbon dioxide
    C. foam   D. ordinary sprinkler

6. According to the Fire Code, the MAXIMUM quantity of calcium carbide which may be lawfully stored without a permit is _____ lbs.

    A. 60   B. 80   C. 100   D. 120

7. A Class C refrigerating system, as defined in the Fire Code, is one in which the quantity of refrigerant does NOT exceed _____ lbs.

    A. 20   B. 25   C. 30   D. 35

8. According to the Building Code, a tank used to provide the required primary water supply to a standpipe system may also be used as a supply for an automatic sprinkler system

    A. in all cases where both have been installed
    B. where there are other acceptable sources of water supply for the sprinkler system
    C. only when the standpipe system has a direct connection to the public water system
    D. provided that its capacity is at least five thousand gallons greater than that required for the sprinkler system

9. For computing the capacity of water supplies other than the fire pump, the Building Code assumes that the average discharge, in gallons per minute, from a standard one-half inch sprinkler head is

    A. 20   B. 25   C. 30   D. 35

10. The door that can be closed to separate the bedrooms from the rest of the apartment is the door between the

    A. entrance hall and the bedroom hall
    B. living room and the entrance hall
    C. kitchen and the living room
    D. dining room and the living room

Questions 11-25.

DIRECTIONS: Questions 11 through 25 are to be answered SOLELY on the basis of the following facts and Building Inspection Form. Each box on the form is numbered. Read the facts and review the form before answering the questions.

Firefighters are required to inspect all buildings within their assigned area of the city. They check conditions within the building for violations of fire safety laws. While inspecting a building, they must fill out a Building Inspection Form as a record of the conditions they observed.

On June 12, 2015, Firefighter Edward Gold, assigned to Engine Company 82, is ordered by Captain John Bailey to inspect the building at 1400 Compton Place as part of the engine company's monthly building inspection duty. The building is a one-story brick warehouse where books of the S & G Publishing Company are stored before shipment to stores.

Firefighter Gold enters the warehouse through the main entrance door in the front of the building. Though an exit sign is present above the door, the sign is unlit because of a burned-out bulb. There is a small office to one side of the main entrance area where Firefighter Gold goes to meet the warehouse manager, Mr. Stevens. The firefighter explains the purpose of the inspection.

Firefighter Gold tells the manager that he will check the automatic sprinkler system first because if a fire got started in a warehouse full of stored books, the fire could spread rapidly. He asks Mr. Stevens for the Certificate of Fitness issued to the company employee certified to maintain the sprinkler system in working order. The certificate is dated June 1, 2002, and Gold observes that it has expired. The manager promises to have the certificate renewed as soon as possible.

The firefighter wants to locate the main control valve of the sprinkler system. He asks Mr. Stevens to go with him and show him its location. Gold and the manager leave through an office door which leads into the main working area of the warehouse. They locate the main sprinkler control valve on the wall in a corner of the work area behind high shelves stocked with books. The firefighter observes that the main control valve is sealed in the open position. Gold next climbs a ladder lying against the storage shelves and measures the distance between the top of the stack of books on the highest shelf and the sprinkler heads suspended on pipes below the ceiling. The distance is three feet.

Firefighter Gold next inspects the remaining exits from the building. A large fire door leads out to the loading dock in the rear of the warehouse. A small door on the side of the warehouse that is used by employees when they leave for the day is partially obstructed by cartons. Lighted exit signs can be clearly seen above both doors. During working hours, only the main entrance door and the fire door to the loading dock are unlocked. Mr. Stevens says he keeps the side door locked to keep employees from leaving early and only unlocks it at closing time.

Firefighter Gold and the manager then walk through the main work area. Gold observes that fireproof rubbish receptacles are placed at frequent intervals. However, they are not covered and the contents are overflowing, resulting in several piles of litter on the floor. *No Smok-*

ing signs are on the walls of the work area, but are difficult to see behind the rows of high storage shelves.

The two fire extinguishers in the work area are found lying on the floor rather than hung on wall racks. The two other fire extinguishers in the warehouse, one in the office and one in the employee lounge, are both correctly hung on wall racks. All four fire extinguishers are fully charged. According to their tags, they were last inspected on March 11, 2015.

Firefighter Gold continues the inspection by checking on the electrical wiring, which appears to be generally in good condition. However, four switch boxes lack covers. The main junction box has a cover, but it cannot be closed because the cover is corroded.

The inspection is now complete, so Firefighter Gold thanks Mr. Stevens for his cooperation and leaves the building. Gold checks that all required information is entered on the Building Inspection Form, including information concerning building violations. Firefighter Gold signs and dates the Building Inspection Form and then submits it to Captain Bailey for his review. After reviewing Firefighter Gold's report, Captain Bailey signs the Building Inspection Form.

BUILDING INSPECTION FORM

DIVISION (1)	BATTALION (2)	COMPANY (3)	
BUILDING INFORMATION	Name of Business (4)		Address (5)
	Type of Business (6)		Occupancy Code Number (7)
CONDITION OF EXITS	Number of Exits (8)	Exits Obstructed (9)	Exits unlocked (10)
	Exit Signs (11)	Exit Sign Lights (12)	Fire Doors (13)
HOUSEKEEPING CONDITIONS	Rubbish Receptacles (14)		No Smoking Signs (15)
	Clearance of stock in Feet from Sprinkler Heads (16)		
	Electrical Wiring (17)	Switches (18)	Junction Box (19)
CONDITION OF FIRE EXTINGUISHERS	Charged (20)	Placement (21)	Date of Last Inspection (22)
CONDITION OF AUTOMATIC SPRINKLER SYSTEM	Color of Siamese (23)	Main Control Valve (24)	Shut-off sign (25)
	Certificate of Fitness (26)		Date of Last Inspection (27)
SPECIAL CONDITIONS	Rubbish/Obstructions (28)		Certificate of Occupancy (29)
			Heavy Load Signs (30)
FIRE DEPARTMENT INFORMATION	Inspector Name_____ Signature _____ (31)	Rank (32)	Date (33)
	Officer Name_____ (34) Signature _____	Rank (35)	Date (36)

11. Which one of the following should be entered in Box 3?   11._____

    A. Ladder Company 79   B. Engine Company 12
    C. Ladder Company 140   D. Engine Company 82

12. Which one of the following should be entered in Box 4? _____ Company.   12._____

    A. G & R Printing   B. S & G Printing
    C. R & G Publishing   D. S & G Publishing

13. Which one of the following should be entered in Box 8?   13._____

    A. 2   B. 3   C. 4   D. 5

14. Which one of the following should be entered in Box 9? _____ door.   14._____

    A. Office   B. Side   C. Main   D. Fire

15. Which one of the following should be entered in Box 10? _____ door and _____ door.   15._____

    A. Fire; main   B. Side; office
    C. Fire; side   D. Main; cellar

16. The entry in Box 12 should show that replacement bulbs are needed for _____ light (s).   16._____

    A. one   B. two   C. three   D. all

17. The entry in Box 14 should show that covers are missing from _____ of the rubbish receptacles.   17._____

    A. two   B. three   C. four   D. all

18. Which one of the following should be entered in Box 16?   18._____

    A. One and one-half   B. Two
    C. Two and one-half   D. Three

19. Which one of the following should be entered in Box 19?   19._____

    A. Faulty circuits   B. Exposed wiring
    C. Corroded cover   D. Good condition

20. Which one of the following entries about the placement of fire extinguishers should appear in Box 21?   20._____

    A. One on the floor; three hung on wall racks
    B. Two on the floor; two hung on wall racks
    C. Three on the floor; one hung on wall rack
    D. Four hung on wall racks

21. Which one of the following should be entered in Box 22?   21._____

    A. June 1, 2012   B. May 21, 2014
    C. March 11, 2015   D. May 1, 2015

22. The entry in Box 24 should show that the position of the main control valve is   22._____

    A. open   B. half open
    C. one-third closed   D. closed

7 (#1)

23. Which one of the following should be entered in Box 26?   23.____

    A. Expired
    B. Missing from file
    C. Never issued
    D. Current

24. Which one of the following should be entered in Box 28?   24.____

    A. Ceiling plaster cracked
    B. Rubbish piles litter work floor
    C. Second floor stairway blocked
    D. Open paint cans on loading dock

25. Which one of the following should be entered in Box 34?   25.____

    A. John Bailey
    B. Edward Gold
    C. John Gold
    D. Edward Bailey

KEY (CORRECT ANSWERS)

1. D	11. D
2. A	12. D
3. D	13. B
4. C	14. B
5. A	15. A
6. D	16. A
7. A	17. D
8. D	18. D
9. A	19. C
10. A	20. B

21. C
22. A
23. A
24. B
25. A

TEST 2

DIRECTIONS: Each question or incomplete statement is followed by several suggested answers or completions. Select the one that BEST answers the question or completes the statement. *PRINT THE LETTER OF THE CORRECT ANSWER IN THE SPACE AT THE RIGHT.*

1. The materials of which a building are constructed and the opportunities for the spread of fire are important, but the GREATEST single hazard is usually that of   1.____

    A. occupancy
    B. location
    C. fire protective measures
    D. construction

2. A warehouse with a leaky roof contains a large amount of building material.   2.____
   The one of the following materials which is MOST likely to set fire to the warehouse is

    A. gasoline
    B. crude oil
    C. lime
    D. kerosene

3. For the most effective results in conducting a Fire Prevention Week campaign, it would be DESIRABLE to emphasize fire prevention   3.____

    A. in its broader community aspects
    B. as a means of lowering insurance rates
    C. as it applies to the individuals' own homes
    D. as a means of lowering operating costs of the fire department

4. Floor or wall openings sometimes prevent the banking up of heated air.   4.____
   This condition, with respect to sprinklers, is considered

    A. advantageous
    B. unimportant
    C. detrimental
    D. good ventilation

5. The BEST all-round fireproofing material, due to its high resistance to heat, its lightness, its great strength, its adaptability to any shape, and which is also very easily repaired when damaged by a severe fire, is   5.____

    A. brick
    B. hollow clay tile
    C. gypsum
    D. concrete

6. Commercial storage and industrial occupancies are classified in the Fire Code as   6.____

    A. highly hazardous
    B. moderately hazardous
    C. lightly hazardous
    D. all of the above

7. An unusually large number of fires of *unknown cause* is characteristic of the fires involving   7.____

    A. restaurants
    B. warehouses
    C. mercantile stores
    D. hospitals

8. It is obvious that where a division wall is not continued through the roof, and where the roof is combustible on both sides of the wall, fire is almost certain to spread beyond the wall if the fire is of any duration. According to the above statement, there is NEED of   8.____

    A. parapets
    B. more resistive division walls
    C. fire-stopping of roof spaces
    D. fire-stopping division walls

9. The hazard of flammable gases is generally _____ to that of flammable liquids. 9._____

   A. opposite   B. dissimilar
   C. similar   D. identical

10. The MOST important factor that would materially decrease large-loss supermarket fires is 10._____

    A. education of the general public
    B. separating the utility area from the rest of the building by a fire-resistive wall
    C. maintenance of an adequate supply of fire extinguishers
    D. keeping all aisles clear of merchandise and storage

11. The PRIMARY difference between the large number of small fires that produces a small percentage of total losses, and the smaller number of large fires that accounts for 95 percent of the total loss in the United States is usually 11._____

    A. the nature of the material involved in the fire
    B. the type of structure involved
    C. early discovery
    D. availability of personnel to fight the fire

12. From the fire prevention standpoint, air conditioning and air blower systems are of concern MAINLY because they 12._____

    A. provide a means for the spread of fire through the building served
    B. severely limit adequate ventilation in case of fire
    C. intensify fires from other sources by providing abnormally large amounts of air
    D. characteristically accumulate hazardous quantities of dust and lints which are subject to spontaneous ignition

13. At what interval of time should rubbish and waste materials be removed from piers, docks, and wharves? 13._____

    A. At least daily
    B. Once per week
    C. As often as needed to prevent dangerous condition
    D. As fast as accumulated

14. Of the various rooms found in the average school building, which two places deserve MORE consideration from a point of view of preventing personal injuries that may result from panic?
    The 14._____

    A. auditorium and the boiler room
    B. classroom on the highest floor and the room in the lowest (basement) part of the building
    C. auditorium and the cafeteria
    D. classroom nearest the auditorium exit and the auditorium itself

15. The underlying reason behind routine periodic and frequent fire prevention inspection is:

    A. Occupants, hazards, and code compliances may vary considerably in given buildings over a short period
    B. The need for favorable public opinion
    C. A large city usually has many new buildings being constructed
    D. Most individuals continually and consciously try to evade the fire regulations

16. The FIRST objective of all fire prevention is

    A. safeguarding life against fire
    B. reducing insurance rates
    C. preventing property damage
    D. confining fire to a limited area

17. Which one of the following is the cause of the GREATEST number of fires?

    A. Electrical wiring
    B. Spontaneous ignition
    C. Sparks on roofs
    D. Smoking and matches

18. The type of occupancy in which the LARGEST number of fires occurs is

    A. restaurants and other mercantile establishments
    B. hospitals, theatres, and other public buildings
    C. dwellings, including apartments and hotels
    D. bakeries, cleaning establishments, and other manufacturing plants

19. Which one of the following factors generally should be given the GREATEST right in estimating the fire risk in a general or mixed public warehouse?

    A. Availability of water hydrants to the warehouse
    B. Location of warehouse with respect to other buildings in the area
    C. Intensity and direction of prevailing winds in the area
    D. Kind of merchandise stored in the warehouse

20. Of the following, the one which is perhaps the MOST important year-round element in fire prevention in residences is

    A. proper and regular disposal of combustible waste
    B. care in the operation of heating systems
    C. periodic inspections by members of the fire department
    D. radio announcements calling attention to fire hazards in the home

21. The fire prevention and fire protection problem resolves itself into three phases, each of which must receive attention. The possibility of human or mechanical failure makes it unsafe to place sole reliance on any one method. If two of these phases are preventing the outbreak of fire and preventing the serious spread of fire, then the third phase would be providing for

    A. extensive research in the cause and prevention of non-incendiary fires
    B. the specialized training of fire department personnel at all levels
    C. the prompt detecting and extinguishing of fire
    D. ample modern firefighting equipment

22. The LARGEST cause of apartment and tenement house fires is

   A. smoking and matches
   B. electrical
   C. gas stoves and explosions
   D. heating equipment

23. Fire loss statistics show that 90 percent of the losses occur at _____ percent of the fires.

   A. 10   B. 15   C. 20   D. 30

24. To best analyze the fire prevention and protection problem in a certain section of the city, the MOST basic thing that is necessary to know is the _____ the area.

   A. number of fire companies in
   B. structural and occupancy data of
   C. number of people living in
   D. available water supply for

25. Of the following, the GREATEST fire hazard in furniture and cabinet shops is

   A. spontaneous ignition
   B. heating systems in buildings
   C. exposure
   D. misuse of electricity

KEY (CORRECT ANSWERS)

1. A		11. C	
2. C		12. A	
3. C		13. A	
4. C		14. C	
5. B		15. A	
6. D		16. A	
7. B		17. D	
8. A		18. C	
9. C		19. D	
10. B		20. A	

21. C
22. A
23. A
24. B
25. A

TEST 3

DIRECTIONS: Each question or incomplete statement is followed by several suggested answers or completions. Select the one that BEST answers the question or completes the statement. *PRINT THE LETTER OF THE CORRECT ANSWER IN THE SPACE AT THE RIGHT.*

1. On inspection of a 5-story building, you find that only half of the required stairways serving the top floor continue to the roof.
   This condition is legal if the building is a(n)

   A. warehouse
   B. school
   C. office building
   D. department store

   1._____

2. In order to determine whether a building in a county is within the fire limits, one of the sources you should check is the maps that are part of the

   A. Administrative Code
   B. most recent zoning resolution
   C. zoning resolution in force
   D. Sanborn maps

   2._____

3. During inspection of a motion picture theatre, you find 6 reels of safety film in closed containers in the manager's office.
   This condition is

   A. *legal* because the film is safety film
   B. *illegal* because film may not be kept in an office
   C. *legal* because there is less than 25,000 feet of film
   D. *illegal* because the film must be kept in a vented metal cabinet

   3._____

4. A two-story, two-family dwelling has been converted to three-family use. There is only one stairway to the street. There is no fire escape. The stairs are not enclosed with fire-regarded partitions. The doors to the apartments are self-closing, but are not fireproof.
   Of the following statements, the one that is MOST complete and accurate is that the condition described

   A. *conforms* to the requirements of the Multiple Dwelling Law
   B. *does not conform* to the requirements of the Multiple Dwelling Law because the apartment doors should be fireproof
   C. *does not conform* to the requirements of the Multiple Dwelling Law because the apartment doors should be fireproof and the stair hall should be enclosed
   D. *does not conform* to the requirements of the Multiple Dwelling Law because the apartment doors should be fireproof, the stair hall should be enclosed, and a second means of egress should be provided

   4._____

5. On fire prevention inspection, you find a revolving door being used as a required means of egress from the lobby of a hospital.
   This condition is

   A. *illegal*
   B. *legal* only if the door is a type A revolving door
   C. *legal* only if the door is a type B revolving door
   D. *legal* only if all other required means of egress are swinging doors

   5._____

6. The time of day when the GREATEST number of fires occur is from

   A. Midnight to 6 A.M.
   B. 6 A.M. to 12 Noon
   C. 12 Noon to 6 P.M.
   D. 6 P.M. to Midnight

7. Of the following types of industrial organizations, the one in which the GREATEST number of fires occur is

   A. newspaper and printing shops
   B. carpet and rug factories
   C. foundries, metal works, and machine shops
   D. paint, oil, and varnish factories

8. The fire department and the United States Coast Guard have agreed on a program for coordinating their fire prevention activities on the city waterfront.
   Part of this agreement provides for notification of the other party whenever

   A. any violation is discovered
   B. any serious violation is discovered
   C. any violation is discovered and is not abated within 10 days
   D. any violation is discovered involving a matter under the jurisdiction of the other party

9. A company on AFID makes a complete inspection of a 12-story commercial building occupied as follows:
   Alpha Co. - floors 1 through 5 and half of 6
   Beta Co. - half of 6 and all of 7
   Delta Co. - part of 8
   Gamma Co. - part of 8
   Epsilon Co. - part of 8
   All other floors - each occupied by single companies According to Regulations, the number of inspections to be recorded on reports for statistical purposes is MOST NEARLY

   A. 12   B. 13   C. 16   D. 18

10. The division coordinator is authorized to discontinue the use of individual inspectors for inspections generally performed by companies on AFID. This action is to be taken when the company

    A. is up to date on its inspection schedule for the year
    B. is 10 percent ahead of its inspection schedule for the year
    C. has completed sufficient number of inspections to assure completion of its schedule for the year
    D. has completed its regular inspection schedule for the year

Questions 11-15.

DIRECTIONS: Column I lists five properties of fire extinguishers. Column II lists various types of fire extinguishers. For each property in Column I, select the fire extinguisher from Column II having that property and place the letter next to the extinguisher in the properly numbered space.

COLUMN I	COLUMN II	
11. Contains aluminum sulphate in solution	A. Water gas cartridge expelled	11._____
12. Water in extinguishing agent will cause corrosion of container	B. Antifreeze (water mixed with antifreeze chemical)	12._____
13. Usually contains sodium chloride	C. Carbon dioxide	13._____
	D. Foam	
14. Produces a mass of bubbles filled with CO_2 gas	E. Carbon tetrachloride	14._____
15. Inspection check by weighing extinguisher only		15._____

16. Of the following categories by means of which structured fires were extended during the last few years, the MOST common involved was

    A. cocklofts   B. partitions
    C. stairways   D. doors

16._____

17. The one of the following which is NOT required by the housing maintenance code for the protection of openings into public halls in old-law tenements less than four stories high is that *every*

    A. door opening into the public hall shall be fireproof, having a fire-resisting rating of at least one hour
    B. door opening into the public hall shall be self-closing
    C. glazed panel in a door opening into a public hall shall be glazed with wire glass
    D. transom opening upon any public hall shall be glazed with wire glass and firmly secured in a closed position

17._____

18. Firestopping of the space above a hung ceiling into areas not exceeding 3,000 square feet is REQUIRED when the

    A. structural members within the concealed space are individually protected with materials having the required fire resistance
    B. concealed space is sprinklered
    C. ceiling contributes to the required fire resistance of the floor or roof assembly
    D. ceiling is not an essential part of the fire-resistive assembly

18._____

19. When a deluge sprinkler system is provided around the perimeter of a theater stage, manual operating devices as well as automatic controls are required by the building code.
The MOST complete and accurate statement concerning these manual operating devices is that they should be located

    A. at the emergency control station
    B. adjacent to one exit from the stage
    C. at the emergency control station and adjacent to one exit from the stage
    D. at the emergency control station, adjacent to one exit from the stage, and at the deluge valve

19._____

20. Yellow painted Siamese caps on office buildings will indicate that the Siamese serves ONLY

   A. the standpipe in pressurized stairs
   B. the sprinklers in sub-basement locations
   C. a combination standpipe and sprinkler system
   D. as a supply line to the fire pump for the upper level standpipe outlets

21. A fireman, on his way to work, is stopped by a citizen who complains that the employees of a nearby store frequently pile empty crates and boxes in a doorway, blocking passage. The one of the following which would be the MOST appropriate action for the fireman to take is to

   A. assure the citizen that the fire department's inspectional activities will eventually *catch up* with the store
   B. obtain the address of the store and investigate to determine whether the citizen's complaint is justified
   C. obtain the address of the store and report the complaint to his superior officer
   D. ask the citizen for specific dates on which this practice has occurred to determine whether the complaint is justified

22. In the Halon coding system, each digit represents the number of atoms while the position of the digit in the number represents a specific chemical element.
    For Halon number 1202, the number 1 indicates that the molecule contains one atom of

   A. bromine   B. carbon   C. chlorine   D. fluorine

23. A street vault incident described in a department safety bulletin explains how two persons were asphyxiated when they descended into the vault.
    Tests of the atmosphere of the vault showed that the hazard was due to

   A. light smoke and flames generated by burning synthetic insulation
   B. gasoline vapors from a leaking underground tank
   C. replacement of oxygen by carbon dioxide
   D. natural gas entering the vault

24. It is sometimes necessary to make a simple field test to determine the flammability of decorative materials.
    Of the following, the one that generally produces the LEAST reliable results when tested by exposure to a small flame is

   A. all-glass fabric
   B. untreated cotton cloth
   C. flame-retardant treated paper
   D. flexible plastic film

25. The one of the following substances with the LEAST tendency to spontaneous heating is

   A. fish meal   B. lamp black
   C. scrap rubber   D. soap powder

KEY (CORRECT ANSWERS)

1.	B	11.	D
2.	C	12.	E
3.	B	13.	B
4.	A	14.	D
5.	A	15.	C
6.	C	16.	B
7.	C	17.	A
8.	B	18.	C
9.	C	19.	C
10.	C	20.	C

21. C
22. B
23. D
24. D
25. B

TEST 4

DIRECTIONS: Each question or incomplete statement is followed by several suggested answers or completions. Select the one that BEST answers the question or completes the statement. *PRINT THE LETTER OF THE CORRECT ANSWER IN THE SPACE AT THE RIGHT.*

1. Every applicant for a certificate of license to install underground gasoline storage tanks is required to 1.____

   A. be a resident of the city and maintain a place of business in the city
   B. file a bond and evidence of liability insurance
   C. be a resident of the city or maintain a place of business in the city
   D. pass a written examination given by the fire department

2. After firing a blast, the licensed blaster at a construction site discovered that one charge had not detonated and the exact direction of the drill hole could not be determined. The licensed blaster under the supervision and orders of the walking boss used a metal scraper to remove the tamping, after which the hole was reloaded and fired. This action 2.____

   A. complies with the Fire Prevention Code
   B. violates the Code because a metal scraper was used
   C. violates the Code because the Fire Commissioner's approval is required before charges are removed
   D. violates the Code because no notification was given to the Division of Fire Prevention concerning the incident

3. The Fire Prevention Code specifies that a special permit is required for each of the following EXCEPT 3.____

   A. refining petroleum collected from oil separators or manufacturing plants
   B. loading of small arms ammunition by hand in a retail store selling ammunition
   C. operating a wholesale drug or chemical house
   D. generating acetylene gas

4. The one of the following that is the MOST acceptable statement concerning the fire protection for the truck loading rack in a bulk oil terminal is that the rack must be equipped with a 4.____

   A. water spray system, automatically controlled
   B. foam system, remote manually controlled
   C. water spray system, remote manually controlled
   D. foam system, automatically controlled

5. A fire insurance inspector suggested to the manager of a fireproof warehouse that bags of flour be stacked on skids (wooden platforms 6" high, 6x6 feet in area).
Of the following, the BEST justification for this suggestion is that, in the event of a fire, the bags on skids are LESS likely to 5.____

   A. topple
   B. be damaged by water used in extinguishment
   C. catch fire
   D. be ripped by fire equipment

6. Permitting piles of scrap paper cuttings to accumulate in a factory building is a bad practice CHIEFLY because they may

   A. ignite spontaneously
   B. interfere with fire extinguishment operations
   C. catch fire from a spark
   D. interfere with escape of occupants if a fire occurs

7. Firefighters are inspecting a furniture factory. During the inspection, they find employees smoking cigarettes in various areas.
   In which area does smoking pose the GREATEST danger of causing a fire?

   A. Employee lounge   B. Woodworking shop
   C. A private office   D. A rest room

8. The MAXIMUM quantity of paints which may be manufactured or stored without a permit, according to the Fire Prevention Code, is _____ gallons.

   A. 20   B. 25   C. 30   D. 50

9. Oil separators are required by the Administrative Code before issuance of a permit to a garage for the storage of volatile inflammable oil if the garage accommodates _____ or more motor vehicles.

   A. four   B. five   C. six   D. ten

10. *The term cellar, as used in the Building Code, shall mean a story having _____ of its height, measured from finished floor to finished ceiling, below the curb level at the center of the street front.*
    The one of the following which, when filled in the blank space, BEST completes the sentence is

    A. more than one-half
    B. no more than one-half
    C. more than three-quarters
    D. no more than three-quarters

11. The Oil Burner Rules of the Board of Standards and Appeals state, *No movable combustible materials shall be stored or maintained within _____ feet of heating apparatus, except where same is protected by fire-retarding material.*
    The one of the following numbers which, when inserted in the blank space above, MOST accurately completes the sentence is

    A. 2   B. 3   C. 4   D. 5

12. As used in the Building Code, the term *horizontal exit* refers to a(n)

    A. exit door on the ground floor which is at the same level as the street grade
    B. corridor or hallway leading to the exit stairs
    C. fire escape with the balcony at the same level as the floor
    D. connection between two floor areas through a fire wall

13. According to the Building Code, a required exit stairway enclosure in a public building MUST have a fire resistance rating of _____ hour(s).

    A. 1   B. 2   C. 3   D. 4

14. A recently enacted section of the Fire Prevention Code places limitations on the use of kerosene-burning equipment.
    When all the provisions of this section of the Code are in full effect, the one of the following uses of kerosene-burning equipment which will NOT be permitted is equipment used exclusively for

    A. cooking purposes
    B. lighting purposes
    C. demonstration and sales purposes
    D. heating purposes in any building in an area not supplied with permanent piped gas

15. The provisions of the Building Code require that in a building more than two stories high, the required stairways must all continue to the roof EXCEPT in a(n)

    A. office building B. school building
    C. theater D. storage warehouse

16. The definition of *non-combustible* in the Building Code was recently amended with regard to acoustical and thermal insulation.
    Which one of the following would be *non-combustible* according to the Code?
    Insulation with a flame-spread rating not greater than _____, smoke-developed rating not greater than _____.

    A. 25; 50 B. 50; 50 C. 50; 75 D. 75; 100

17. A new school dormitory is two stories and less than thirty feet in height. Inspection reveals that there is only one stairway from the second floor and the maximum travel distance to the stair enclosure is 80 feet. The stair enclosure and corridors are provided with automatic sprinkler protection.
    With respect to the provisions of the Building Code as it applies to this situation, it would be MOST appropriate to state that this building

    A. complies with the Code
    B. does not comply with the Code because the maximum travel distance is excessive
    C. does not comply with the Code because two exits remote from each other on each story are lacking
    D. does not comply with the Code because the sprinkler system was not extended into the rooms

18. Of the following statements, the one that is LEAST in accord with the material and equipment requirements for oil spill control at bulk storage plants and petroleum product pipelines is that

    A. all material and equipment must be of a type acceptable to the Fire Commissioner
    B. dispersants should be used only when directed by the fire department, Coast Guard, or Corps of Engineers
    C. pipeline operators shall provide at least one vacuum truck
    D. the minimum amount of absorbent material at any plant shall be 2,000 pounds

19. In a high-rise office building over 100 feet in height, the doors opening into interior stair enclosures may NOT be locked from either side at intervals of four stories or less EXCEPT where

    A. the building is equipped with an approved automatic sprinkler system
    B. the doors are equipped with an automatic fail-safe system for opening doors
    C. the second means of egress is a standard fire tower
    D. every floor of the building has a fire warden on duty

19._____

20. The Rules of the Board of Standards and Appeals require that combustible materials used for decorative purposes within special occupancy structures be made flameproof. Approval of flameproof materials is

    A. valid for an indefinite period
    B. limited to a period of 6 months
    C. limited to a period of 1 year
    D. limited to a period of 2 years

20._____

21. *A multiple dwelling, according to the Multiple Dwelling Law, is a dwelling occupied as the residence of _____ or more families living independently of each other.*
    The one of the following numbers which, when inserted in the blank space above, MOST accurately completes the sentence is

    A. 2   B. 3   C. 4   D. 5

21._____

22. The one of the following statements that is MOST accurate is that in multiple dwellings, windows at grade levels at sidewalks, yards, or courts may

    A. not have bars
    B. have bars provided that they are easily removed from the inside of the window
    C. have bars but at least one window in each room must be without bars
    D. have bars but at least one window in each apartment must be without bars

22._____

23. The number of extra sprinkler heads which must be kept in the premises of a building with an automatic sprinkler system, according to the Building Code, is

    A. 10
    B. 10 percent of the number of sprinkler heads in the entire system
    C. 6
    D. 6 percent of the number of sprinkler heads in the entire system

23._____

24. The Building Code requires that standpipe systems be equipped with pressure reducing valves where the normal hydrostatic pressure at a 2 1/2" hose outlet valve exceeds _____ lbs. per square inch.

    A. 50   B. 55   C. 60   D. 65

24._____

25. Walls of structures used for public entertainment may be covered with combustible wall coverings, according to the Building Code, provided that the

    A. wall covering is pasted or cemented directly to the plaster surfaces of the wall
    B. wall covering does not extend more than six feet in height
    C. building is a Class 1 fireproof structure
    D. building has a seating capacity of 600 people or less

25._____

KEY (CORRECT ANSWERS)

1.	C	11.	D
2.	A	12.	D
3.	D	13.	C
4.	C	14.	D
5.	B	15.	B
6.	C	16.	A
7.	B	17.	A
8.	A	18.	B
9.	B	19.	B
10.	A	20.	C

21. B
22. D
23. C
24. B
25. A

EXAMINATION SECTION
TEST 1

DIRECTIONS: Each question or incomplete statement is followed by several suggested answers or completions. Select the one that BEST answers the question or completes the statement. *PRINT THE LETTER OF THE CORRECT ANSWER IN THE SPACE AT THE RIGHT.*

1. During an inspection of a plant which manufactures paper products, the officer observes completed work being placed in paper cartons. The cartons are then stacked on wooden skids in a separate storage area awaiting shipment.
   The one of the following which is generally the MOST appropriate evaluation of the practice described in this situation is that skids

   A. are highly combustible, adding much fuel to the fire
   B. permit excess air flow to fires
   C. minimize water damage losses by raising stock off the floor
   D. provide space under the stock, thus permitting fire to be more readily extinguished

   1.____

2. Assume that a three-story, Class 3 non-fireproof building has been converted to two-family use. There is one stairway to the street, 2'8" wide. The doors to the apartments all swing in. There are no fire escapes.
   The one of the following statements that is MOST accurate is that the situation as described

   A. complies with all applicable laws
   B. is illegal because the stairs are too narrow
   C. is illegal because two means of egress are required
   D. is illegal because the doors do not swing in the direction of egress

   2.____

3. The flammability limits of aviation fuels are of little significance in understanding their fire hazard properties CHIEFLY because the fuels

   A. have practically the same limits
   B. form flammable vapor-air mixtures at all temperatures
   C. ignite readily under tank failure conditions
   D. resist flashing to vapor when in the gelled form

   3.____

4. An inspector enters a luncheonette and discovers that the owner, the only person on duty, apparently does not understand English.
   The one of the following which would be the BEST action for the inspector to take in this situation is to attempt to

   A. make the owner understand by speaking English in a loud, clear voice
   B. make the owner understand by using sign language
   C. find a customer or passerby who can act as an interpreter
   D. question the owner closely to determine whether he really does not understand English

   4.____

5. For proper protection of low flash point flammable liquid processes, automatic sprinkler protection with a strong water supply is essential.
   The BEST justification of this statement is that

   5.____

A. a sprinkler system with a strong water supply will extinguish most fires involving such processes
B. water from sprinklers will reduce the intensity of burning of the liquid and the danger to exposures
C. although the sprinklers are ineffective on flammable liquid fires, they provide protection in the event of other types of fires
D. water from the sprinklers will dilute the flammable liquid and make extinguishment easier

6. According to the regulations, company commanders shall cause a thorough inspection of all schools within their administrative district.
Such inspections shall be made

   A. annually
   B. semi-annually
   C. at the beginning of each school term
   D. within 60 days after school opens for the fall term

6._____

7. While inspecting a garage, a fire inspector notices that a garage license has not been issued for the premises by the Department of Licenses.
The inspector should

   A. discontinue his inspection pending a determination by the Department of Licenses of the allowable motor vehicle occupancy
   B. complete his inspection and forward it (including a statement of the allowable motor vehicle occupancy) with a request that a copy be sent to the Department of Licenses
   C. discontinue his inspection and request that a communication (inquiry form) be sent to the Department of Licenses asking for an explanation
   D. complete his inspection and forward it with a request that the Department of Licenses be asked to determine the allowable motor vehicle occupancy

7._____

Questions 8-11.

DIRECTIONS: Questions 8 through 11 are to be answered on the basis of the information given in the following paragraph.

The principal value of inspection work is in the knowledge obtained relating to the various structural features of the building and the protective features provided. Knowledge of the location of stairways and elevators, the obstruction provided by merchandise, the danger from absorption of water by baled stock, the potential hazard of rupture of containers such as drums or cylinders, and the location of protective equipment, all are essential features to be noted and later discussed in company school and officer's college.

8. According to the above paragraph, the CHIEF value of inspection work is to gather information which will aid in

   A. fixing responsibility for fires
   B. planning firefighting operations
   C. training new firemen
   D. obtaining compliance with the Building Code

8._____

9. The one of the following objects which would be the MOST help in accomplishing the objective of the inspection as stated in the above paragraph is a

   A. copy of the Building Code
   B. chemical analysis kit
   C. plan of the building
   D. list of the building's tenants

10. An example of a *structural feature* contained in the above paragraph is the

    A. location of stairways and elevators
    B. obstruction provided by merchandise
    C. danger of absorption of water by baled stock
    D. hazard of rupture of containers such as drums or cylinders

11. Of the following, the BEST example of what is meant by a *protective feature,* as used in the above paragraph, is

    A. a fire extinguisher
    B. a burglar alarm
    C. fire insurance
    D. a medical first-aid kit

12. When a violation order is to be served and the owner or person in charge of the premises cannot readily be located, every effort shall be made to serve such order. Of the following statements concerning the attempts to serve such an order, the one that is NOT correct is:

    A. Attempt to ascertain from occupants or people in the area the name and address of the owner or management
    B. Send a member to effect service if the owner or management is located in the city but out of the company district
    C. Make an appointment by telephone for service of the order
    D. Post the violation notice prominently in or on the premises and mail a copy to the owner or management

13. Every applicant for a certificate of license to install underground gasoline storage tanks is required to

    A. be a resident of the city and maintain a place of business in the city
    B. file a bond and evidence of liability insurance
    C. be a resident of the city or maintain a place of business in the city
    D. pass a written examination given by the fire department

14. The Fire Prevention Code specifies that a special permit is required for each of the following EXCEPT

    A. refining petroleum collected from oil separators or manufacturing plants
    B. loading of small arms ammunition by hand in a retail store selling ammunition
    C. operating a wholesale drug or chemical house
    D. generating acetylene gas

15. The one of the following that is the MOST acceptable statement concerning the fire protection for the truck loading rack in a bulk oil terminal is that the rack must be equipped with a

A. water spray system, automatically controlled
B. foam system, remote manually controlled
C. water spray system, remote manually controlled
D. foam system, automatically controlled

16. The one of the following which is NOT in accord with the regulations for the use of Halon 1301, extinguishing agent, is that

    A. maximum concentration shall not exceed 10 percent where human habitation is present in the volume to be flooded
    B. minimum concentration of FE 1301 used shall not be less than 10 percent
    C. a discharge rate which results in attaining the design concentration in 8 seconds is acceptable
    D. a central office connection must be provided for fire detection or systems operating where human habitation is present in the volume to be flooded

17. Members of the uniformed force are authorized to issue summonses where fire perils exist, although it is generally preferable to first issue a violation order to correct the illegal condition.
    However, members must issue a summons immediately in a licensed place of public assembly upon noting

    A. an obstructed revolving exit door in a crowded cabaret
    B. the absence of a certified standpipe system operator in a theatre
    C. an inoperative fire extinguishing system in a restaurant cooking duct
    D. standees in a motion picture theatre

18. During the course of an inspection at a blasting site, an officer notes that the magazine has been provided with electrical security devices, and that it contains eight 10-pound cartons of explosives which are to be stored overnight, overhead wires run from the magazine to the watchman's shanty, and the driller, without a C. of F., loads holes under the direct supervision of the blaster. The condition as described is generally ILLEGAL because

    A. explosives must be in original and unbroken packages of 50 or 25 pound capacity only
    B. storage of explosives between the hours of 10 P.M. and 6 A.M. is prohibited
    C. all electrical wiring must be protected by heavy wall conduit and be buried at least 12 inches deep
    D. no person may load holes in blasting operations unless they hold a certificate of fitness

19. The one of the following that is LEAST in accord with the regulations for the use of Halon 1301 extinguishing agent systems is that

    A. these systems are limited to applications as automatic total flooding systems for interior Class B and C fires and Class A fires that are not deep-seated
    B. abort systems are permitted for smoke detector activated systems which provide the manual capacity to *dump* the Halon 1301 immediately
    C. actuation of only one products-of-combustion device will fail to initiate the *dump* of Halon 1301 but will actuate the local and central office company alarms
    D. concentrations used shall not exceed 10 percent in areas where human habitation is present in the volume to be flooded

20. Interstate transportation of petroleum products into and through the city in tank trucks which do NOT conform to fire department requirements is GENERALLY

   A. *not permitted* even when the pickups are all made outside the city and no pickups are made in the city
   B. *permitted* without restriction if the vehicles comply with United States Department of Transportation regulations governing interstate commerce
   C. *not permitted* where deliveries are to be made in the city
   D. *permitted* during non-business hours, along regularly established commercial routes

21. Of the following occupancies constructed and occupied in 1962, each of which accommodates less than 300 persons, the one that CANNOT be described as a *place of assembly*, according to the applicable building code, is a

   A. college assembly hall
   B. motion picture theatre
   C. courtroom
   D. legitimate theatre

22. According to the labor law, the one of the following conditions that is generally considered to be LEGAL in a 5-story building constructed and occupied as a factory since 1911 is that

   A. a single means of egress is provided from a floor of 2500 sq.ft. or less where no person is regularly employed
   B. no point on the upper floor which is equipped with an approved sprinkler system is more than 200 feet distant from an exit
   C. one of the two required stairways extends to the roof from which there is egress to an adjacent building
   D. there are double swinging doors leading to an exit on an upper floor where more than 5 persons are employed

23. Certain old factory buildings may be found to have some fire escapes which are not in accordance with the requirements of the labor law.
It is generally CORRECT to state of these substandard factory exits that they

   A. may be used in computing occupancy exit requirements if maintained in good repair and the building is equipped with an automatic sprinkler
   B. must be provided with a counterbalanced stairway in lieu of the former drop ladder in guides
   C. shall be kept clear of all obstructions and periodically used during required fire drills
   D. may not be equipped with any exit or directional sign at the openings leading thereto

24. According to the labor law, the use of plate glass in fire windows in fireproof buildings is

   A. *prohibited*, except in buildings less than 75 feet in height
   B. *permitted*, if the fire windows are located more than 30 feet horizontally from the nearest opening in the wall of another building
   C. *prohibited* for use in all fire windows in fireproof buildings
   D. *permitted* if the fire windows are more than 30 feet above the roof of a building within a horizontal distance of 25 feet

25. Under certain conditions, a newsstand may be located in a street floor lobby which serves as an exit passageway for a building constructed after 1976.
The one of the following which is NOT one of these conditions is that the newsstand must

    A. occupy no more than 100 square feet or 5 percent of the net floor area of the lobby, whichever is greater
    B. not reduce the clear width of the lobby at any point
    C. be located at least 30 feet from an exit door
    D. be protected by at least 2 automatic sprinkler heads if constructed of combustible material

25.____

KEY (CORRECT ANSWERS)

1. C	11. A
2. A	12. D
3. C	13. C
4. C	14. D
5. B	15. C
6. A	16. B
7. D	17. C
8. B	18. D
9. C	19. D
10. A	20. D

21. C
22. B
23. A
24. B
25. B

TEST 2

DIRECTIONS: Each question or incomplete statement is followed by several suggested answers or completions. Select the one that BEST answers the question or completes the statement. *PRINT THE LETTER OF THE CORRECT ANSWER IN THE SPACE AT THE RIGHT.*

1. Suppose that a factory has stored within it a number of substances. 1.____
   If the owner asked you which of the following is MOST likely to constitute a fire hazard, you would reply

   A. sodium chloride   B. calcium chloride
   C. chromium   D. silicon dioxide

2. Vertical openings, such as dumbwaiters, elevators, and chutes, are the bane of a fire- 2.____
   fighting force.
   This condition arises MAINLY because the existence of such openings in a burning building facilitates

   A. accidental falls   B. generation of gases
   C. spread of the fire   D. the perpetration of arson

3. Suppose that a neighbor were to ask you whether there is more hazard in the use of ker- 3.____
   osene than gasoline at ordinary room temperature.
   You should reply that there is MORE hazard in the use of

   A. *kerosene,* because it gives off dangerous quantities of explosive vapors which are lighter than air
   B. *gasoline,* because gasoline vapor may flow along the floor and be ignited at a long distance from its point of origin
   C. *kerosene,* because its flash point is very low
   D. *gasoline,* particularly because when ignited it burns

4. Steel supporting beams in buildings often are surrounded by a thin layer of concrete to 4.____
   keep the beams from becoming hot and collapsing during a fire.
   The one of the following statements which BEST explains how collapse is prevented by this arrangement is that concrete

   A. becomes stronger as its temperature is increased
   B. acts as an insulating material
   C. protects the beam from rust and corrosion
   D. reacts chemically with steel at high temperatures

5. It has been suggested that property owners should be charged a fee each time the Fire 5.____
   Department is called to extinguish a fire on their property.
   Of the following, the BEST reason for *rejecting* this proposal is that

   A. delay in calling the Fire Department may result
   B. many property owners don't occupy the property they own
   C. property owners may resent such a charge as they pay real estate taxes
   D. it may be difficult to determine on whose property a fire started

6. An officer inspecting buildings in a commercial area came to one whose outside surface appeared to be of natural stone. The owner told the officer that it was not necessary to inspect his building as it was *fireproof*. The officer, however, completed his inspection of the building.
Of the following, the BEST reason for continuing the inspection is that

   A. stone buildings catch fire as readily as wooden buildings
   B. the Fire Department cannot make exceptions in its inspection procedures
   C. the building may have been built of imitation stone
   D. interiors and contents of stone buildings can catch fire

7. From the viewpoint of fire safety, the CHIEF advantage of a foam rubber mattress compared to a cotton mattress is that the foam rubber mattress

   A. is slower burning
   B. generates less heat when burning
   C. does not smolder
   D. is less subject to water damage

8. At a social gathering, a fire chief hears a man who describes himself as the owner of the XYZ factory state that he *pays off* fire department inspectors who visit his establishment. When the chief asks the man whether he will repeat his statement under oath, the man refuses with the remark, *I am not looking for trouble.*
In this situation, the chief should

   A. forget the incident since the factory owner is not willing to give evidence
   B. investigate the background and reputation of the man to determine whether he really owns the factory and has any reason for making false statements about the fire department
   C. report the incident to police authorities
   D. report the incident to higher authorities in the fire department

9. The one of the following methods of storing large piles of coal which is undesirable because it increases the danger of spontaneous heating is

   A. making the pile compact by use of a roller
   B. storing the coal on smooth, solid ground
   C. covering the sides and top of the pile with road tar
   D. mixing coal of various sizes in one pile

10. The one of the following materials which has the LEAST tendency to spontaneous heating is

    A. baled hides
    B. bagged charcoal
    C. bulk fish scrap
    D. boxed mineral wool

11. In most buildings in which lighting is provided by artificial means and an auxiliary system for emergency exit lighting is not provided, phosphorescent exit and directional signs are required.
Of the following occupancies, the one which is generally EXCLUDED from this requirement is a

    A. warehouse
    B. school dormitory
    C. hospital
    D. library

12. In determining overcrowding or adequacy of means of egress, a fire officer must be aware that the minimum number of persons to be provided for in any floor area shall be the number which can be accommodated within the net floor area at a given occupancy and area per person.
Accordingly, the GREATEST concentration of persons to be provided for will be generally found in a

    A. basement sales area
    B. high school classroom
    C. dance hall
    D. work room

13. Of the following statements, the one that is generally ACCURATE concerning the installation of combustible luminous suspended ceilings is that they may

    A. not be installed below an existing suspended ceiling
    B. be installed below existing sprinkler heads
    C. not be used in any room in occupancy group F (assembly)
    D. be installed in corridors not exceeding 100 sq.ft.

14. The building code exempts from the sprinkler requirements those floors which are generally unventilated but are equipped with a given openable area.
A fixed window will be considered openable if it is

    A. equipped with an interior heat sensitive device to actuate the automatic fire shutters
    B. of frangible glass panels and located 15 feet below grade
    C. within 8 feet of an openable window of at least 3 feet x 3 feet dimension
    D. readily broken and not more than 110 feet above grade

15. Of the following, the MOST complete and accurate statement about exit requirements is that there shall be at least two door openings, remote from each other and leading to exits from every room or enclosed space, in a business occupancy (E) in which the total occupant load *exceeds*

    A. 25   B. 50   C. 75   D. 100

16. On October 23, 1976, 25 persons died and many were injured as a result of an arson fire in an illegal social club in the Bronx.
Of the following, the MOST probable contributory cause of this multiple loss of life was the

    A. door to the club was not self-closing and was opened in the direction of egress when the fire occurred
    B. front windows had been bricked-up and prevented access by department ladders
    C. confusing layout caused many patrons to bypass the secondary means of egress and become trapped in the toilet rooms
    D. original lath and plaster had been replaced by combustible wood paneling and there had been an extensive use of highly flammable decorations

17. It is INCORRECT for a fire officer giving training on the protection of electronic data processing (EDP) units and ancillary equipment against fire damage to state that

A. the design features of EDP units make them relatively resistant to damage by temperatures under 600° F
B. smoke and acids produced by fire can adversely affect the operation of computer equipment and magnetic components
C. the heat and steam produced by a fire and its extinguishment that would not normally damage ordinary paper records may easily damage magnetic tapes
D. in cases where fire can spread throughout or beyond the computer's housing, a fixed CO_2 system may be required

18. Of the following exit and access requirements relating to dead-end corridors in various occupancy group buildings, it is generally MOST accurate to state that

    A. no more than one classroom shall be permitted on a dead-end corridor in an educational occupancy
    B. storage of combustible materials in non-combustible lockers is permitted in dead-end corridors in an institutional occupancy
    C. dead-end corridors are not permitted in an assembly occupancy
    D. no more than one patient bedroom is permitted in a dead-end corridor in an institutional occupancy

19. In the past, building marquee collapses have resulted in the injury or death of firefighters. According to the new building code, marquees are generally

    A. not permitted
    B. permitted if supported by incombustible piers at the curb line
    C. not permitted to project beyond the street line
    D. permitted on buildings of a public nature but may have to be removed if the building occupancy is changed

20. When a standpipe system is altered, extended, or extensively repaired, it must undergo certain inspections and tests.
    Of the following, it is generally MOST accurate to state that the

    A. entire system shall be subjected to the hydrostatic test pressure
    B. altered, new or repaired section shall be subjected to the pressure test and the entire system subjected to the flow test
    C. flow test shall be confined to a determination that water is available at the top outlet of each riser
    D. pressure test in buildings not exceeding 3 stories or 40 feet in height need only sustain 150 percent of the normal hydrostatic pressure at the topmost hose outlet

21. A substance which is subject to *spontaneous combustion* is one that

    A. is explosive when heated
    B. is capable of catching fire without an external source of heat
    C. acts to speed up the burning of material
    D. liberates oxygen when heated

Questions 22-25.

DIRECTIONS: Questions 22 through 25 are to be answered on the basis of the following paragraph.

5 (#2)

For the five-year period 2006-2010, inclusive, the average annual fire loss in the United States amounted to approximately $1,354,830,000. Included in this estimate is $1,072,666,000 damage to buildings and contents, and $282,164,000 average annual loss in aircraft, motor vehicles, forest and other miscellaneous fires not involving buildings. Preliminary estimates indicate that the total United States fire loss in 2011 was $1,615,000,000. These are property damage fire losses only and do not include indirect losses resulting from fires which are just as real and sometimes far more serious than property damage losses. But because evaluation of indirect monetary losses is usually very difficult, their importance in the national fire waste picture is often overlooked.

22. According to the data in the above paragraph, the BEST of the following estimates of the total direct fire loss in the United States for the six-year period 2006-2011, inclusive, is

    A. $1,400,000,000
    B. $2,700,000,000
    C. $7,000,000,000
    D. $8,400,000,000

23. The BEST example of an indirect fire loss, as that term is used in the above paragraph, is monetary loss due to

    A. smoke or water damage to exposures
    B. condemnation of foodstuffs following a fire
    C. interruption of business following a fire
    D. forcible entry by firemen operating at a fire

24. Suppose that during the period 2011-2015 the average annual fire loss to buildings and contents increases 10 percent, and the average annual loss due to fires not involving buildings decreases 10 percent. The MOST valid of the following conclusions is that the average annual fire loss for the 2011-2015 period, compared to the losses for the 2006-2011 period,

    A. will increase
    B. will decrease
    C. will be unchanged
    D. cannot be calculated from the information given

25. If a comparison is made between total annual direct and indirect fire losses on the basis of the information given in the above paragraph, the MOST valid of the following conclusions is that

    A. generally, direct losses are higher
    B. generally, indirect losses are higher
    C. generally, direct and indirect losses are approximately equal
    D. there is not sufficient information to determine which is higher or if they are approximately equal

KEY (CORRECT ANSWERS)

1. D
2. C
3. B
4. B
5. A

6. D
7. C
8. D
9. D
10. D

11. D
12. A
13. C
14. A
15. D

16. A
17. C
18. A
19. D
20. C

21. B
22. D
23. C
24. A
25. D

TEST 3

DIRECTIONS: Each question or incomplete statement is followed by several suggested answers or completions. Select the one that BEST answers the question or completes the statement. *PRINT THE LETTER OF THE CORRECT ANSWER IN THE SPACE AT THE RIGHT.*

1. It has been suggested that companies be given additional Apparatus Field Inspection Duty and other inspectional duties as punishment for poor performance of evolutions, poor condition of equipment or quarters, etc.
   Of the following, the MOST valid objection to this proposal is that

   A. the punishment does not directly improve the skills or functions which are found to be deficient
   B. inspectional activities would be degraded by making such assignments a form of punishment
   C. the punishment is imposed on a group rather than on an individual basis
   D. scheduling of regular inspectional activities would be disrupted

   1.____

2. The Administrative Code authorizes members to issue summonses in cases arising under laws relating to fires and to fire peril.
   Departmental regulations require that such summonses be returnable in the appropriate court _____ than 14 calendar days, _____ Sundays and holidays.

   A. not less; including   B. not less; excluding
   C. not more; including   D. not more; excluding

   2.____

3. When conducting an Apparatus Field Inspection of an occupancy with a required and approved sprinkler system, it is MOST important, of the following, for firemen to make certain that

   A. feeder lines are adequate to supply the number of sprinkler heads
   B. sprinkler heads are sufficient and properly spaced
   C. stock does not interfere with the proper distribution of water from sprinkler heads
   D. records of monthly hydrostatic pressure tests are properly kept and are up to date

   3.____

4. While inspecting an above-ground storage tank installation, an inspector notices leakage of the contents through *weep* holes in a tank.
   This is a sign that the

   A. tank contents are under excessive pressure
   B. strength of the entire tank may be endangered by corrosion
   C. volumetric capacity of the tank has been exceeded
   D. tank is *breathing* as intended

   4.____

5. A member on inspectional duty came across, in a building under construction, a propane gas heater with its safety valve negated by means of wire and tape across the buttons at the top of the safety assembly.
   Of the following actions taken by the member in this situation, the one that is NOT in accord with departmental orders is the

   5.____

77

A. serving of a violation order to discontinue use of devices to negate safety features on propane gas heaters on premises
B. picking up of the permits for storage and use of propane
C. notification of the Battalion Chief of the administrative district concerned
D. impounding of the propane heater

6. Of the following, the PRIMARY purpose of holding fire tests at a high-rise office building is to 6.____

    A. determine the hazard of polyurethane insulation
    B. evaluate the effectiveness of sprinklers with a limited water supply
    C. test the effectiveness of stair pressurization
    D. develop procedures for venting the fire floor by window vents

7. At the first sign of a fire, the manager of a motion picture theatre had the lights turned on and made the following announcement: *Ladies and gentlemen, the management has found it necessary to dismiss the audience. Please remain seated until it is time for your aisle to file out. In leaving the theatre, follow the directions of the ushers. There is no danger involved.* 7.____
The manager's action in this situation was

    A. *proper*
    B. *improper,* chiefly because he did not tell the audience the reason for the dismissal
    C. *improper,* chiefly because he did not permit all members of the audience to leave at once
    D. *improper,* chiefly because he misled the audience by saying that there was no danger

8. Generally, sprinkler heads must be replaced each time they are used. 8.____
The BEST explanation of why this is necessary is that the sprinkler heads

    A. are subject to rusting after discharging water
    B. may become clogged after discharging water
    C. have a distorted pattern of discharge of water after use
    D. are set off by the effect of heat on metal and cannot be reset

9. A fire insurance inspector suggested to the manager of a fireproof warehouse that bags of flour be stacked on skids (wooden platforms 6" high, 6x6 feet in area). Of the following, the BEST justification for this suggestion is that in the event of a fire, the bags on skids are less likely to 9.____

    A. topple
    B. be damaged by water used in extinguishment
    C. catch fire
    D. be ripped by fire equipment

10. Permitting piles of scrap paper cuttings to accumulate in a factory building is a bad practice CHIEFLY because they may 10.____

    A. ignite spontaneously
    B. interfere with fire extinguishment operations
    C. catch fire from a spark or smoldering match
    D. interfere with escape of occupants if a fire occurs

11. High grass and weeds should not be permitted to grow near a building CHIEFLY because, in the event of a grass fire, the weeds and grass may

   A. give off toxic fumes
   B. limit maneuverability of firemen
   C. interfere with the escape of occupants from the building
   D. bring the fire to the building and set it on fire

11.____

12. Visitors near patients in *oxygen tents* are not permitted to smoke.
The BEST of the following reasons for this prohibition is that

   A. the flame of the cigarette or cigar may flare dangerously
   B. smoking tobacco is irritating to persons with respiratory disease
   C. smoking in bed is one of the major causes of fires
   D. diseases may be transmitted by means of tobacco smoke

12.____

13. A MAJOR difference between the building code currently in effect and the one in effect prior to it is that in the current code

   A. doors to the outside grade must be the same size as corridor doors
   B. sprinklering of a building will permit a reduction in total door width
   C. the width of an exit door is based on the width of the corridor leading to it
   D. the width of exit doors is based on both the number of persons and the type of occupancy

13.____

14. While inspecting a one-story factory building erected in 1962, you notice that an exit door has been relocated. The size, location, and lighting of all exits in the building comply with the old building code in effect before.
To determine whether the relocated exit is a legal one, it is necessary to check the provisions of

   A. the State Labor Law and the new building code for the relocated exit *only*
   B. the State Labor Law *only*
   C. the new building code for the relocated exit *only*
   D. none of the foregoing since checking the old building code is sufficient

14.____

15. The new building code divides the construction clauses into two major construction groups.
These two groups are called

   A. fireproof and non-fireproof
   B. rigid frame and flexible frame
   C. commercial and residential
   D. combustible and noncombustible

15.____

16. The State Labor Law requires that the balconies and stairways of outside fire escapes be able to safely sustain a live load, in pounds per square foot, of _____ with a safety factor of _____.

   A. 75; two   B. 90; four   C. 105; two   D. 120; four

16.____

17. A plant manufacturing nitro-cellulose products has 100 employees. The Fire Prevention Code requires that these premises be equipped with fire pails filled with water. The required MINIMUM number of such pails must be

    A. 25 B. 50 C. 75 D. 100

18. The MAIN purpose of an oil separator is to

    A. separate volatile inflammable oils from other oils
    B. provide a fireproof block between a spark or flame device and an oil storage tank
    C. prevent volatile inflammable oils from flowing into a sewer
    D. make it impossible for the wrong kind of oil to be delivered from a bulk storage plant

19. The MAXIMUM quantity of fuel oil permitted to be stored in an exposed tank in the cellar of a two-family dwelling is _____ gallons.

    A. 225 B. 550 C. 750 D. 875

20. According to the Fire Prevention Code, the MAXIMUM quantity of paint (other than water base) that may be stored without a permit is _____ gallons.

    A. 10 B. 15 C. 20 D. 25

21. Of the following licenses, certificates of qualification, or certificates of fitness, the Fire Department does NOT issue the one authorizing the holder to

    A. operate refrigerating machines (unlimited capacity)
    B. install underground storage tanks for gasoline
    C. operate low pressure boilers using #6 oil
    D. install oil burning equipment

22. In the course of your work in a residential area, you see a wood frame, brick veneer dwelling, two-stories and attic in height, erected in 1965. The building is occupied by two families, with a living room in the attic.
    Without special approval by the Board of Standards and Appeals, this condition could

    A. not be legal
    B. be legal provided that there is a fire escape from the attic
    C. be legal provided the stair enclosure is properly fire retarded
    D. be legal provided that the attic living room is not used as a bedroom

23. A typical occupancy falling into the Assembly occupancy group as used in the building code would be a

    A. radio station   B. library
    C. nursing home   D. tavern

24. Of the following situations, the one in which a fire escape may NOT be considered a legal means of egress is in a three-story

    A. factory building erected in 1912
    B. mixed occupancy building with a store on the first floor and one family on each of the floors above, erected in 1965
    C. multiple dwelling erected in 1971
    D. office building erected in 1950 and altered in 1972

25. A storage garage is one that has 25.____
   A. a stock room for repair parts for vehicles
   B. an area for vehicles that are not used on a daily basis
   C. a gasoline tank to supply gasoline to the vehicles
   D. room only for vehicles that are to be sold

KEY (CORRECT ANSWERS)

1. B	11. D
2. A	12. A
3. C	13. D
4. B	14. B
5. A	15. D
6. C	16. B
7. A	17. B
8. D	18. C
9. B	19. B
10. C	20. C

21. D
22. A
23. D
24. C
25. C

TEST 4

DIRECTIONS: Each question or incomplete statement is followed by several suggested answers or completions. Select the one that BEST answers the question or completes the statement. *PRINT THE LETTER OF THE CORRECT ANSWER IN THE SPACE AT THE RIGHT.*

1. A violation order is to be served requiring the immediate removal of liquefied petroleum gas cylinders when such cylinders are found on construction sites without a permit issued by the Fire Department.
   Pending removal of such cylinders,

   A. vacate procedures are to be instituted
   B. a fireman is to be detailed to the site to safeguard the illegally stored gas cylinders
   C. the contractor is to be ordered to provide a watchman to safeguard the illegally stored gas cylinders
   D. the Police Department is to be notified so that a patrolman can be assigned to the site to safeguard the illegally stored gas cylinders

   1.____

2. A four-story loft building is now occupied as follows: Street level - furniture repair and refinishing shop; 2nd story - one apartment occupied by an artist-in-residence, wife, and 5 young children; 3rd story - two apartments each occupied by an artist-in-residence and his wife; 4th story - one apartment occupied by an artist-in-residence, his wife, and his mother-in-law. The building is non-fireproof construction, 40' x 70', is 50' in height, and has an automatic wet sprinkler system protecting the furniture shop. The occupancy as described is

   A. *legal*
   B. *illegal,* because the sprinkler system does not extend throughout the building
   C. *Illegal,* because the number of occupants exceeds the permissible limits
   D. *illegal,* because of the presence of the furniture repair and refinishing shop

   2.____

3. Some organizations have adopted the National Fire Protection Association diamond-shaped coding system for identifying characteristics of hazardous materials. The diamond shown in the diagram at the right has its boxes labeled W, X, Y, and Z.
   Under the National Fire Protection Association coding system, the lettered boxes represent, respectively,

   A. X - Health, Y - Reactive, W - Flammable
   B. X - Reactive, Y - Flammable, W - Health
   C. X - Health, Y - Reactive, Z - Flammable
   D. X - Flammable, Y - Health, Z - Reactive

   3.____

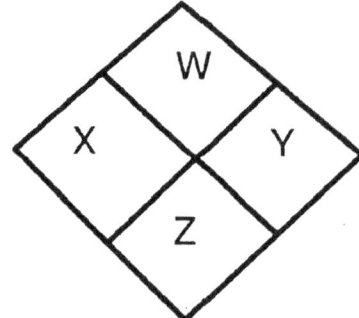

4. The shut sprinkler control valve is one of industry's greatest fire hazards. When it is necessary to shut down a system for repairs or other reasons, certain precautions should be taken.
Of the following statements regarding such precautions, the LEAST acceptable is to

   A. have the system shut down during non-working hours
   B. have the system shut down during working hours while normal operations are going on
   C. notify the Fire Department of the intended shutdown
   D. prepare to supply the system through the two-inch drain in the event of an emergency or fire

Questions 5-8.

DIRECTIONS: Questions 5 through 8 are to be answered on the basis of the information given in the following paragraph.

A mixture of a combustible vapor and air will burn only when the proportion of fuel to air lies within a certain range, i.e., between the upper and lower limits of flammability. If a third, non-combustible gas is now added to the mixture, the limits will be narrowed. As increasing amounts of diluent are added, the limits come closer until, at a certain critical concentration, they will converge. This is the peak concentration. It is the minimum amount of diluent that will inhibit the combustion of any fuel-air mixture.

5. If additional diluent is added beyond the peak concentration, the flammable limits of the mixture will

   A. converge rapidly
   B. diverge slowly
   C. diverge rapidly
   D. not be affected

6. If the four numbers listed below were peak concentration values obtained in a test of four diluents, then the MOST efficient diluent would have the value of

   A. 7.5   B. 10   C. 12.5   D. 15

7. The word *inhibit,* as used in the last sentence of the above paragraph, means MOST NEARLY

   A. slow the rate of
   B. prevent entirely the occurrence of
   C. reduce the intensity of
   D. retard to an appreciable extent the manifestation of

8. The one of the graphs shown below which BEST represents the process described in the paragraph is

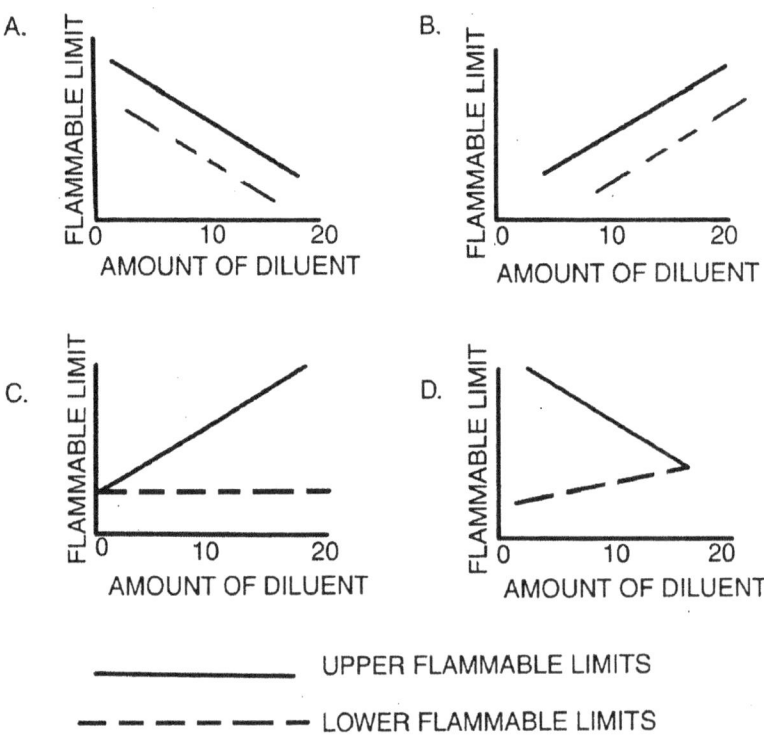

———————— UPPER FLAMMABLE LIMITS

— — — — — — LOWER FLAMMABLE LIMITS

9. Of the following metals, the one which is LEAST acceptable as a non-sparking metal for tools is 9.___

    A. hardened copper
    B. bronze
    C. brass
    D. copper alloys

10. Of the heating defects responsible for hotel fires, the MAJOR defect is 10.___

    A. defective flues
    B. overheated appliances
    C. defective appliances
    D. inadequate clearance

11. Community relations and fire prevention education efforts must be concentrated in residential neighborhoods, particularly in the depressed areas of the city.
The one of the following which does NOT provide support for this point of view is that 11.___

    A. residential occupants are exposed to more serious occupancy hazards than industrial workers
    B. open hydrants, excessive false alarms, and hostile acts are concentrated in depressed areas
    C. rubbish fires and vacant building fires are most frequent in these areas
    D. the primary incidence of fire takes place in residential areas

12. The State Multiple Dwelling Law allows a *family* to have four boarders, and the City Multiple Dwelling Law allows a *family* to have only two boarders.
In the city, a *family* is allowed 12.___

A. two boarders because the Multiple Dwelling Code is the more restrictive requirement
B. four boarders because the State law takes precedence over the city code
C. two or four boarders, depending upon whether the Law or Code applies to a given situation
D. two or four boarders, at the discretion of the Fire Commissioner

13. Fire Department regulations governing the issuance of city-wide permits for the use of combustible gases during temporary torch operations require fire guards to make inspections after completion of torch operations for the purpose of detecting fire. Signed inspection reports are to be filed and available for examination by the Fire Department.
The one of the following which is MOST accurate and complete is that such inspections are to be made _____ after completion of operations.

    A. every 15 minutes, for a period of one hour,
    B. one-half hour and one hour
    C. every half hour, for a period of two hours,
    D. one half hour, one hour, and two hours,

14. On an A.F.I.D., a company comes upon the following garages:
    I. Adjacent to a dwelling occupied by one family, storing two cars, one owned by the family and the other by the next door neighbor who pays a monthly rental
    II. In a dwelling outside the fire limits, occupied by one family storing three cars owned by the family
    III. In a fireproof dwelling occupied by three families in two stories above the garage, with two means of egress and no entrances to any apartment through the garage, storing two cars owned by tenants

    A Fire Department permit is required for

    A. none of these garages   B. garages I and III
    C. garages II and III   D. all three garages

15. If a building is altered under the provisions of the building code, and the building is not provided with sprinkler protection, the one of the following actions that the company officer should take is to

    A. transmit an A-8 report for referral to the Department of Buildings
    B. issue a summons to the owner of the building
    C. prepare a report on Department letterhead and send it to the Division of Fire Prevention
    D. call the Department of Buildings and notify them about the violation

16. The one of the following fibers that can be made into fabric which can be effectively treated with common water-soluble-salt flame-retardant solutions is

    A. dacron   B. nylon   C. rayon   D. nomex

17. The inspection of public assembly occupancies classified as theatres in company administrative districts should be scheduled so that each such premises is inspected AT LEAST once every

    A. 30 days, approximately one half hour before scheduled performances
    B. 30 days, at irregular time periods when premises are open to the public

C. three months, approximately one half hour before scheduled performances
D. three months, at irregular time periods when premises are open to the public

18. The one of the following automatic fire alarm detectors that works on the principle of uneven expansion of bi-metallic strips is the _____ device.

    A. rate compensation
    B. ionization type
    C. rate of rise type
    D. fixed temperature

19. The one of the following which is probably the MOST frequent source of ignition of flammable vapors in hospital operating rooms is

    A. static electricity
    B. x-ray equipment
    C. sterilizing machinery
    D. electric cauterizing devices

20. At an open demonstration, polyurethane foam, widely used in furniture, was exposed to fire.
    In this demonstration, it was shown that the foam

    A. was self-extinguishing
    B. flamed and gave off acrid smoke
    C. could not be ignited
    D. melted but would not flame

Questions 21-23.

DIRECTIONS: Questions 21 through 23 are to be answered on the basis of the following paragraph.

Shafts extending into the top story, except those stair shafts where the stairs do not continue to the roof, shall be carried through and at least two feet above the roof. Every shaft extending above the roof, except open shafts and elevator shafts, shall be enclosed at the top with a roof of materials having a fire resistive rating of one hour and a metal skylight covering at least three-quarters of the area of the shaft in the top story, except that skylights over stair shafts shall have an area not less than one-tenth the area of the shaft in the top story, but shall be not less than fifteen square feet in area. Any shaft terminating below the top story of a structure and those stair shafts not required to extend through the roof shall have the top enclosed with materials having the same fire resistive rating as required for the shaft enclosure.

21. The above paragraph states that the elevator shafts which extend into the top story are

    A. not required to have a skylight but are required to extend at least two feet above the roof
    B. neither required to have a skylight nor to extend above the roof
    C. required to have a skylight covering at least three-quarters of the area of the shaft in the top story and to extend at least two feet above the roof
    D. required to have a skylight covering at least three-quarters of the area of the shaft in the top story but are not required to extend above the roof

22. The one of the following skylights which meets the requirements of the above paragraph is a skylight measuring

   A. 4' x 4' over a stair shaft which, on the top story, measures 20' x 9'
   B. 4 1/2' x 3 1/2' over a pipe shaft which, on the top story, measures 5' x 4'
   C. 2 1/2' x 1 1/2' over a dumbwaiter shaft which, on the top story, measures 2 1/2' x 2 1/2'
   D. 4' x 3' over a stair shaft which, on the top story, measures 15' x 6'

22._____

23. Suppose that in a Class I building, a shaft which does not go to the roof is required to have a three-hour fire resistive rating.
   In regard to the material enclosing the top of this shaft, the above paragraph

   A. states that a one-hour fire resistive rating is required
   B. states that a three-hour fire resistive rating is required
   C. implies that no fire resistive rating is required
   D. neither states nor implies anything about the fire resistive rating

23._____

Questions 24-25.

DIRECTIONS: Questions 24 and 25 are to be answered SOLELY on the basis of the following passage.

The four different types of building collapses are as follows:

1. <u>Building Wall Collapse</u> - An outside wall of the building collapses but the floors maintain their positions.

2. <u>Lean-to Collapse</u> - One end of a floor collapses onto the floor below it. This leaves a sheltered area on the floor below.

3. <u>Floor Collapse</u> - An entire floor falls to the floor below it but large pieces of machinery in the floor below provide spaces which can provide shelter.

4. <u>Pancake Collapse</u> - A floor collapses completely onto the floor below it, leaving no spaces. In some cases, the force of this collapse causes successive lower floors to collapse.

24. The MOST serious injuries are likely to occur at _____ collapses.

   A. pancake   B. lean-to
   C. floor   D. building wall

24._____

25. Of the following, a floor collapse is MOST likely to occur in a(n)

   A. apartment building   B. private home
   C. factory building   D. hotel

25._____

26. When using a standardized survey report during AFID, it generally is NOT advisable to make an inspection of the facilities in the strict sequence of the items on the form PRIMARILY because the

   A. sequence of the items in the form may not correspond to the physical arrangement of the occupancy or structure
   B. members performing inspection duty will be more likely to make errors of omission rather than commission on the forms

26._____

C. occupancy or structure may require a multi-inspector, multi-page form inspectional approach
D. procedure does not permit distribution of tasks among all the members participating in the inspection

27. Sparks given off by welding torches are a serious fire hazard.
The BEST of the following methods of dealing with this hazard is to conduct welding operations only

   A. in fireproof buildings protected by sprinkler systems
   B. out-of-doors on a day with little wind blowing
   C. on materials certified to be non-combustible by recognized testing laboratories
   D. after loose combustible materials have been cleared from the area and with a man standing by with a hose line

28. Two types of steel hoops are commonly found on older wooden gravity tanks - round hoops and flat ones.
The one of the following statements concerning such hoops that is MOST accurate is that hidden corrosion is a serious problem with _____ hoops.

   A. the round hoops but not with the flat
   B. the flat hoops but not with the round
   C. both types of
   D. neither type of

29. While on AFID, you come across a clothing factory which shows evidence of poor housekeeping practices.
For you to imply to the owner that the Fire Department will conduct frequent inspections of his premises until satisfactory conditions are maintained is

   A. *proper,* mainly because the owner may be persuaded by it to maintain satisfactory conditions
   B. *improper,* mainly because the owner may feel that he is being harassed
   C. *proper,* mainly because any means which result in the elimination of hazardous conditions are permissible
   D. *improper,* mainly because threats which may not be carried out should not be made

30. Generally, officers on fire prevention inspection duty do not inspect the living quarters of private dwellings unless the occupants agree to the inspection.
The BEST of the following explanations of why private dwellings are excluded from compulsory inspections is that

   A. private dwellings seldom catch fire
   B. fires in private dwellings are more easily extinguished than other types of fires
   C. people may resent such inspections as an invasion of privacy
   D. the monetary value of private dwellings is lower than that of other types of occupancies

KEY (CORRECT ANSWERS)

1.	C	11.	A	21.	A
2.	D	12.	A	22.	B
3.	A	13.	B	23.	B
4.	B	14.	B	24.	A
5.	D	15.	A	25.	C
6.	A	16.	C	26.	A
7.	B	17.	A	27.	D
8.	D	18.	D	28.	B
9.	C	19.	A	29.	A
10.	A	20.	B	30.	C

EXAMINATION SECTION
TEST 1

DIRECTIONS: Each question or incomplete statement is followed by several suggested answers or completions. Select the one that BEST answers the question or completes the statement. *PRINT THE LETTER OF THE CORRECT ANSWER IN THE SPACE AT THE RIGHT.*

1. A television receiver has a greater inherent fire hazard than a conventional radio receiver because 1.____

   A. of greater electrical leakage
   B. cabinets are inadequately ventilated
   C. higher voltage is used in the system
   D. they are operated for longer periods of time
   E. the coaxial cable lead-in is covered with a highly flammable coating

2. Of the following, the MOST frequent factor contributing to conflagrations in the United States and Canada in the last 25 years has been 2.____

   A. high winds
   B. lack of exposure protection
   C. delayed alarms
   D. congestion of hazardous occupancies
   E. inadequate water distribution system

3. If, upon reinspection of a plant which has 30 days to comply with a previous order, you find that the order has not been completely obeyed but that some work has taken place, you should 3.____

   A. report to proper authorities to obtain legal action
   B. assume the delay is unavoidable and check again in 30 days
   C. inform the person in charge that a 10-day extension will be granted and that legal action will be taken if the order has not been followed
   D. none of the above

4. An analysis of loss records in one city showed that one-third of the total loss in building fires was in residence buildings and that, of the total loss in such buildings, in the year under study, nearly 80 percent was in multiple dwelling buildings.
The one of the following courses of action for the fire department which should be taken *immediately* on the basis of this report is to 4.____

   A. relocate companies
   B. recommend sprinkler protection for multiple dwellings
   C. institute special training fighting multiple dwelling fires
   D. reduce the protection given to other than multiple dwelling residences
   E. inspect multiple dwellings more thoroughly

5. It is good practice to so install heating devices that under conditions of maximum heat (long-continued exposure) they will not cause the temperature of exposed woodwork to exceed 160° F.
This practice is 5.____

A. *correct* because of the possibility that wood and other combustible materials, after long-continued exposure to relatively moderate heat, may ignite at temperatures far below their usual ignition temperatures
B. *not correct* because no wood in ordinary use will ignite at a temperature of less than 400° F. and, consequently, the requirement is needlessly severe
C. *correct* because oxidation proceeds much more rapidly at higher temperatures
D. *not correct* because oxidation proceeds much more slowly at higher temperatures
E. *correct* because, under prolonged heating, the temperature of the air in the room will build up until the ignition point is reached unless the applied temperature is kept sufficiently low

6. Analysis of the causes of fires is important, as only by knowing the causes of fires is it possible to effectively prevent fire.
An analysis of fires in rooms used for spraying flammable paints and finishes has shown that the MOST important of the following causes is

    A. smoking by employees
    B. defective electrical equipment
    C. spontaneous ignition of paint deposits, rubbish, wiping rags
    D. static electricity resulting from friction
    E. cutting and welding operations

7. The flammability or combustibility of radioactive materials has little or no direct effect on the fire hazard of a laboratory PRIMARILY because

    A. the unusual structural characteristics of such a laboratory serve to limit possible fire spread from such hazards
    B. water or water spray are effective on most radioactive substances
    C. the quantities of such material in any one laboratory are usually small
    D. laboratory fire prevention and firefighting facilities usually exceed maximum fire hazards
    E. such materials are inherently of a low order of combustibility

8. Comparison of the burning qualities of foam rubber and cotton mattresses shows that, generally,

    A. a cotton mattress burns faster but cooler
    B. a foam rubber mattress burns slower but hotter
    C. a foam rubber mattress burns faster and hotter
    D. a cotton mattress burns faster and hotter
    E. the potential fire hazard of a foam rubber mattress is higher

9. During Christmas and other holiday shopping seasons, it is required that frequent inspections shall be made of department stores, at irregular intervals.
Of the following, the MOST important reason for this inspection procedure is to

    A. prevent unnecessary interference with store operations
    B. check characteristic holiday operations
    C. permit more frequent and thorough coverage of the stores in question
    D. avoid delay in urgent fire operations
    E. permit more flexible scheduling of inspection

10. The fire load computation of a building indicates, for the most part, the

    A. risk of a fire breaking out
    B. rate at which a fire is likely to grow
    C. combustibility of the various parts of the building rather than its contents
    D. amount of combustibles and the method of protection
    E. maximum fire stress to which the building might be subjected

11. It is far more important that escape routes from multistory buildings should be protected against smoke and hot gases than from direct flame or heat.
    This statement is

    A. *not correct*; resistive construction is likely to be smoke-resistive as well
    B. *correct*; adequate means for ventilation is essential to prevent cutting off escape routes
    C. *not correct*; unless corridors and escape stairs are constructed of fire resistive materials, progress of fire cannot be blocked
    D. *correct*; unless properly protected from smoke and hot gases, escape stairs would be unusable by occupants
    E. *not correct*; unless properly protected against direct flame or heat, escape routes cannot resist smoke or hot gases

12. The minimum width of exit usually required for a single file of persons is MOST NEARLY _____ inches.

    A. 15-17   B. 18-20   C. 21-23   D. 24-27   E. 27-30

13. The MOST pronounced method of reducing the fire and life hazards in public buildings is by

    A. ample exits of any type
    B. ample stairways inside the buildings
    C. the use of exit signs and panic locks
    D. fire-resisting construction suitable for the occupancy

14. From all viewpoints, the MOST hazardous materials that could be stored, constituting a life as well as a fire hazard, would be

    A. second-hand niter bags
    B. used motor vehicles
    C. loose or baled vegetable fibers
    D. pyroxylin and pyroxylin plastic products

15. The CHIEF fire hazard of welding and cutting operations is

    A. flames of the torch igniting nearby material
    B. broken hose line
    C. flying sparks
    D. back-firing of torch

16. Of the following items associated with motion picture theatres, the PRIMARY hazard is

    A. misuse of electricity   B. heating defects
    C. smoking and matches   D. projection booth fires

17. The MOST hazardous method of fumigation is by the use of

    A. heat (125° F.)
    B. carbon tetrachloride mixture with flammable fumigant
    C. carbon dioxide mixture with flammable fumigant
    D. carbon bisulphide

18. The combined use of inspections, periodic reports of activities, follow-up procedures, special reports from subordinates, and a rating system comprise a system of

    A. coordination   B. command
    C. control   D. representation
    E. on-the-job training

19. What should be provided in air conditioning ducts to *prevent* the spread of fire and smoke through a property?

    A. Automatic dampers   B. Intake screens
    C. Steel wool air filters D. Heat actuated devices

20. The *outstanding* fire hazard of boarding and rooming houses is

    A. misuse of electricity B. smoking and matches
    C. heating defects   D. incendiary

21. The SIMPLEST and MOST feasible method of avoiding the overheating of woodwork near any high temperature heating appliance is by

    A. filling the intervening space with insulating material
    B. covering the woodwork with sheet metal
    C. providing an air space between the woodwork and the appliance
    D. covering the woodwork with asbestos sheets

22. The PRINCIPAL source of fire hazard in connection with heating equipment in mercantile buildings comes from

    A. defective wiring
    B. insufficient clearance from combustible materials
    C. the storage and handling of fuel
    D. defective motors

23. More ink has been spilled on the item of smoking as a cause of fire than on any other, but the total result has been negligible.
    This situation is BEST accounted for by the fact that

    A. smoking is generally an automatic act performed unthinkingly
    B. truly effective facilities for elimination of smoking hazards are exceedingly cumbersome or expensive
    C. most people regard smoking as a personal prerogative and resent control measures
    D. smoking is practiced by many individuals with defective intelligence and social attitudes

24. There are two basic factors in assessing building construction from the fire prevention standpoint. One is the combustibility of materials.
The other is

   A. extinguishment facilities
   B. excess structural strength
   C. ventilation control
   D. limitation of fire spread
   E. means of access and egress

24.____

25. The LEAST accurate statement concerning the protection of openings in walls and partitions is:

   A. Protection of wall openings may prevent either the horizontal or the vertical spread of fire
   B. The general features of a building have no bearing on the extent to which such protection is necessary
   C. The protection secured by fire doors and fire windows cannot be better than the fire resistant value of the walls
   D. Good solid walls are preferable to those with fire doors in restricting the spread of fire

25.____

KEY (CORRECT ANSWERS)

1.	C		11.	D
2.	A		12.	C
3.	A		13.	D
4.	E		14.	D
5.	A		15.	C
6.	C		16.	D
7.	C		17.	D
8.	C		18.	C
9.	B		19.	A
10.	E		20.	C

21. C
22. B
23. A
24. D
25. B

TEST 2

DIRECTIONS: Each question or incomplete statement is followed by several suggested answers or completions. Select the one that BEST answers the question or completes the statement. *PRINT THE LETTER OF THE CORRECT ANSWER IN THE SPACE AT THE RIGHT.*

1. The materials of which a building are constructed and the opportunities for the spread of fire are important, but the GREATEST single hazard is usually that of   1.___

    A. occupancy
    B. location
    C. fire protective measures
    D. construction

2. A warehouse with a leaky roof contains a large amount of building material. The one of the following materials which is MOST likely to set fire to the warehouse is   2.___

    A. gasoline   B. crude oil   C. lime   D. kerosene

3. For the most effective results in conducting a Fire Prevention Week campaign, it would be DESIRABLE to emphasize fire prevention   3.___

    A. in its broader community aspects
    B. as a means of lowering insurance rates
    C. as it applies to the individuals' own homes
    D. as a means of lowering operating costs of the fire department
    E. as a means of assuring the uninterrupted operation of busines

4. Floor or wall openings sometimes prevent the banking up of heated air. This condition, with respect to sprinklers, is considered   4.___

    A. advantageous
    B. unimportant
    C. detrimental
    D. good ventilation

5. The BEST all-round fireproofing material, due to its high resistance to heat, its lightness, its great strength, its adaptability to any shape, and which is also very easily repaired when damaged by a severe fire, is   5.___

    A. brick
    B. hollow clay tile
    C. gypsum
    D. concrete

6. Commercial storage and industrial occupancies are classified in the Fire Code as _____ hazardous.   6.___

    A. highly
    B. moderately
    C. lightly
    D. all of the above

7. An unusually large number of fires of *unknown cause* is characteristic of the fires involving   7.___

    A. restaurants
    B. warehouses
    C. mercantile stores
    D. hospitals

8. It is obvious that where a division wall is not continued through the roof, and where the roof is combustible on both sides of the wall, fire is almost certain to spread beyond the wall if the fire is of any duration. According to the foregoing statement, there is *need* of   8.___

    A. parapets
    B. more resistive division walls
    C. fire-stopping of roof spaces
    D. fire-stopping division walls

9. The hazard of flammable gases is generally _____ to that of flammable liquids. The above missing word is

   A. opposite   B. dissimilar   C. similar   D. identical

10. The MOST important factor that would materially decrease large-loss supermarket fires is

    A. education of the general public
    B. separating the utility area from the rest of the building by a fire-resistive wall
    C. maintenance of an adequate supply of fire extinguishers
    D. keeping all aisles clear of merchandise and storage
    E. fireproof disposal containers for matches, cigarettes, etc. in the sales area

11. The PRIMARY difference between the large number of small fires that produces a small percentage of total losses, and the smaller number of large fires that accounts for 95 percent of the total loss in the United States is usually

    A. the nature of the material involved in the fire
    B. the type of structure involved
    C. early discovery
    D. availability of personnel to fight the fire
    E. availability of adequate apparatus

12. From the fire prevention standpoint, air conditioning and air blower systems are of concern MAINLY because they

    A. provide a means for the spread of fire through the building served
    B. severely limit adequate ventilation in case of fire
    C. intensify fires from other sources by providing abnormally large amounts of air
    D. characteristically accumulate hazardous quantities of dust and lints which are subject to spontaneous ignition

13. At what interval of time should rubbish and waste material be removed from piers, docks, and wharves?

    A. At least daily
    B. Once per week
    C. As often as needed to prevent dangerous conditions
    D. As fast as accumulated

14. Of the various rooms found in the average school building, which two places deserve MORE consideration from a point of view of preventing personal injuries that may result from panic?
    The

    A. auditorium and the boiler room
    B. classroom on the highest floor and the room in the lowest (basement) part of the building
    C. auditorium and the cafeteria
    D. classroom nearest the auditorium exit and the auditorium itself

15. The underlying reason behind routine periodic and frequent fire-prevention inspection is: 15.___

    A. Occupants, hazards, and code compliances may vary considerably in given buildings over a short period
    B. The need for favorable public opinion
    C. A large city usually has many new buildings being constructed
    D. Most individuals continually and consciously try to evade the fire regulations

16. The FIRST objective of all fire prevention is 16.___

    A. safeguarding life against fire
    B. reducing insurance rates
    C. preventing property damage
    D. confining fire to a limited area

17. Which one of the following is the cause of the GREATEST number of fires? 17.___

    A. Electrical wiring
    B. Spontaneous ignition
    C. Sparks on roofs
    D. Smoking and matches

18. The type of occupancy in which the LARGEST number of fires occurs is 18.___

    A. restaurants and other mercantile establishments
    B. hospitals, theatres, and other public buildings
    C. dwellings, including apartments and hotels
    D. bakeries, cleaning establishments, and other manufacturing plants

19. Which one of the following factors generally should be given the GREATEST right in estimating the fire risk in a general or mixed public warehouse? 19.___

    A. Availability of water hydrants to the warehouse
    B. Location of warehouse with respect to other buildings in the area
    C. Intensity and direction of prevailing winds in the area
    D. Kind of merchandise stored in warehouse

20. Of the following, the one which is perhaps the MOST important year-round element in fire prevention in residences is 20.___

    A. proper and regular disposal of combustible waste
    B. care in the operation of heating systems
    C. periodic inspections by members of the fire department
    D. radio announcements calling attention to fire hazards in the home

21. The fire-prevention and fire-protection problem resolves itself into three phases, each of which must receive attention. The possibility of human or mechanical failure makes it unsafe to place sole reliance on any one method. 21.___
    If two of these phases are preventing the outbreak of fire and preventing the serious spread of fire, then the third phase would be providing for

    A. extensive research in the cause and prevention of non-incendiary fires
    B. the specialized training of fire department personnel at all levels
    C. the prompt detecting and extinguishing of fires
    D. ample modern firefighting equipment

22. The LARGEST cause of apartment and tenement house fires is 22.____

    A. smoking and matches
    B. electrical
    C. gas stoves and explosions
    D. heating equipment

23. Fire-loss statistics show that 90 percent of the losses occur at _____ percent of the fires. 23.____

    A. 10   B. 15   C. 20   D. 30

24. To best analyze the fire prevention and protection problem in a certain section of the city, the MOST basic thing that is necessary to know is the _____ the area. 24.____

    A. number of fire companies in
    B. structural and occupancy data of
    C. number of people living in
    D. available water supply for

25. Of the following, the GREATEST fire hazard in furniture and cabinet shops is 25.____

    A. spontaneous ignition
    B. heating systems in buildings
    C. exposure
    D. misuse of electricity

KEY (CORRECT ANSWERS)

1. A		11. C	
2. C		12. A	
3. C		13. A	
4. C		14. C	
5. B		15. A	
6. D		16. A	
7. B		17. D	
8. A		18. C	
9. C		19. D	
10. B		20. A	

21. C
22. A
23. A
24. B
25. A

READING COMPREHENSION
UNDERSTANDING AND INTERPRETING WRITTEN MATERIAL

EXAMINATION SECTION
TEST 1

DIRECTIONS: Each question or incomplete statement is followed by several suggested answers or completions. Select the one that BEST answers the question or completes the statement. *PRINT THE LETTER OF THE CORRECT ANSWER IN THE SPACE AT THE RIGHT.*

Questions 1-4.

DIRECTIONS: Questions 1 through 4 are to be answered SOLELY on the basis of the following paragraph.

The canister-type gas mask consists of a tight-fitting face piece connected to a canister containing chemicals which filter toxic gases and smoke from otherwise breathable air. These masks are of value when used with due regard to the fact that two or three percent of gas in air is about the highest concentration that the chemicals in the canister will absorb and that these masks do not provide the oxygen which is necessary for the support of life. In general, if flame is visible, there is sufficient oxygen for firefighters although toxic gases may be present. Where there is heavy smoke and no flame, an oxygen deficiency may exist. Fatalities have occurred where filter-type canister masks have been used in attempting rescue from manholes, wells, basements, or other locations deficient in oxygen.

1. If the mask described above is used in an atmosphere containing oxygen, nitrogen, and carbon monoxide, we would expect the mask to remove from the air breathed

   A. the nitrogen only
   B. the carbon monoxide only
   C. the nitrogen and the carbon monoxide
   D. none of these gases

2. According to the above paragraph, when a fireman is wearing one of these masks at a fire where flame is visible, he can GENERALLY feel that as far as breathing is concerned, he is

   A. *safe*, since the mask will provide him with sufficient oxygen to live
   B. *unsafe*, unless the gas concentration is below 2 or 3 percent
   C. *safe*, provided the gas concentration is above 2 or 3 percent
   D. *unsafe*, since the mask will not provide him with sufficient oxygen to live

3. According to the above paragraph, fatalities have occurred to persons using this type gas mask in manholes, wells, and basements because

   A. the supply of oxygen provided by the mask ran out
   B. the air in those places did not contain enough oxygen to support life
   C. heavy smoke interfered with the operation of the mask
   D. the chemicals in the canister did not function properly

4. The following shorthand formula may be used to show, in general, the operation of the gas mask described in the above paragraph:
(Chemicals in canister) →(Air + gases) = Breathable Air.
The arrow in the formula, when expressed in words, means MOST NEARLY

   A. replace
   B. are changed into
   C. act upon
   D. give off

Questions 5-7.

DIRECTIONS: Questions 5 through 7 are to be answered SOLELY on the basis of the following paragraph.

The only openings permitted in fire partitions, except openings for ventilating ducts, shall be those required for doors. There shall be but one such door opening unless the provision of additional openings would not exceed in total width of all doorways 25 percent of the length of the wall. The minimum distance between openings shall be three feet. The maximum area for such a door opening shall be 80 square feet, except that such openings for the passage of motor trucks may be a maximum of 140 square feet.

5. According to the above paragraph, openings in fire partitions are permitted ONLY for

   A. doors
   B. doors and windows
   C. doors and ventilation ducts
   D. doors, windows, and ventilation ducts

6. In a fire partition 22 feet long and 10 feet high, the MAXIMUM number of doors 3 feet wide and 7 feet high is

   A. 1   B. 2   C. 3   D. 4

7.

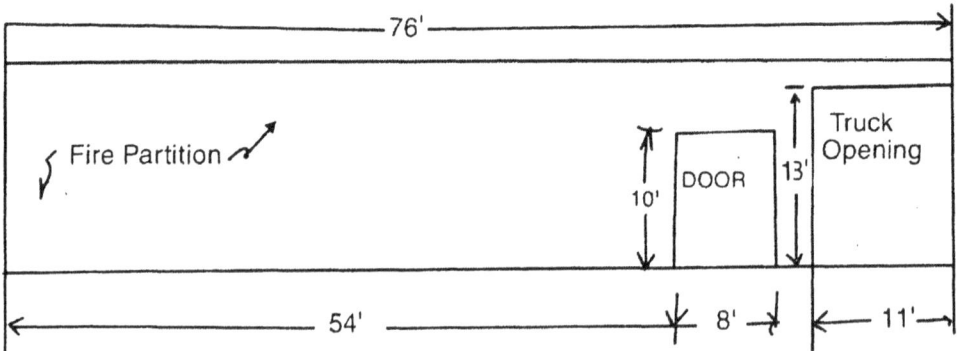

The one of the following statements about the layout shown above that is MOST accurate is that the

A. total width of the openings is too large
B. truck opening is too large
C. truck and door openings are too close together
D. layout is acceptable

Questions 8-11.

DIRECTIONS: Questions 8 through 11 are to be answered SOLELY on the basis of the following paragraph.

Division commanders shall arrange and maintain a plan for the use of hose wagons to transport members in emergencies. Upon receipt of a call for members, the deputy chief of the division from whom the men are called shall have the designated hose wagon placed out of service and prepared for the transportation of members. Hose wagons shall be placed at central assembly points, and members detailed instructed to report promptly to such locations equipped for fire duty. Hose wagons designated shall remain at regular assignments when not engaged in the transportation of members.

8. Preparation of the hose wagon for this special assignment of transporting of members would MOST likely involve

    A. checking the gas and oil, air in tires, and mechanical operation of the apparatus
    B. removal of hose lines to make room for the members being transported
    C. gathering of equipment which will be needed by the members being transported
    D. instructing the driver on the best route to be used

9. Hose wagons used for emergency transportation of members are placed out of service because they are

    A. not available to respond to alarms in their own district
    B. more subject to mechanical breakdown while on emergency duty
    C. engaged in operations which are not the primary responsibility of their division
    D. considered reserve equipment

10. Of the following, the BEST example of the type of emergency referred to in the above paragraph is a(n)

    A. fireman injured at a fire and requiring transportation
    B. subway strike which prevents firemen from reporting for duty
    C. unusually large number of false alarms occurring at one time
    D. need for additional manpower at a fire

11. A *central assembly point*, as used in the above paragraph, would MOST likely be a place

    A. close to the place of the emergency
    B. in the geographical center of the division
    C. easily reached by the members assigned
    D. readily accessible to the intersection of major highways

Questions 12-14.

DIRECTIONS: Questions 12 through 14 are to be answered SOLELY on the basis of the following paragraph.

A plastic does not consist of a single substance, but is a blended combination of several. In addition to the resin, it may contain various fillers, plasticizers, lubricants, and coloring material. Depending upon the type and quantity of substances added to the binder, the properties, including combustibility, may be altered considerably. The flammability of plastics depends upon the composition and, as with other materials, upon their physical size and condition. Thin sections, sharp edges, or powdered plastics will ignite and burn more readily than the same amount of identical material in heavy sections with smooth surfaces.

12. The one of the following conclusions that is BEST supported by the above paragraph is that the flammability of plastics

    A. generally is high
    B. generally is moderate
    C. generally is low
    D. varies considerably

13. According to the above paragraph, *plastics* can BEST be described as

    A. a trade name
    B. the name of a specific product
    C. the name of a group of products which have some similar and some dissimilar properties
    D. the name of any substance which can be shaped or molded during the production process

14. According to the above paragraph, all plastics contain a

    A. resin
    B. resin and a filler
    C. resin, filler, and plasticizer
    D. resin, filler, plasticizer, lubricant, and coloring material

Questions 15-18.

DIRECTIONS: Questions 15 through 18 are to be answered SOLELY on the basis of the following paragraph.

To guard against overheating of electrical conductors in buildings, an overcurrent protective device is provided for each circuit. This device is designed to open the circuit and cut off the flow of current whenever the current exceeds a predetermined limit. The fuse, which is the most common form of overcurrent protection, consists of a fusible metal element which when heated by the current to a certain temperature melts and opens the circuit.

15. According to the above paragraph, a circuit which is NOT carrying an electric current is a(n)

    A. open circuit
    B. closed circuit
    C. circuit protected by a fuse
    D. circuit protected by an overcurrent protective device other than a fuse

16. As used in the above paragraph, the one of the following which is the BEST example of a *conductor* is a(n)

    A. metal table which comes in contact with a source of electricity
    B. storage battery generating electricity
    C. electrical wire carrying an electrical current
    D. dynamo converting mechanical energy into electrical energy

17. A fuse is NOT

    A. an overcurrent protective device
    B. the most common form of overcurrent protection
    C. dangerous because it allows such a strong flow of electricity that the wires carrying it may become heated enough to set fire to materials in contact with them
    D. a safety valve

18. According to the above paragraph, the MAXIMUM number of circuits that can be handled by a fuse box containing 6 fuses

    A. is 3
    B. is 6
    C. is 12
    D. cannot be determined from the information given in the above Paragraph

Questions 19-21.

DIRECTIONS: Questions 19 through 21 are to be answered SOLELY on the basis of the following paragraph.

Unlined linen hose is essentially a fabric tube made of closely woven linen yarn. Due to the natural characteristics of linen, very shortly after water is introduced, the threads swell after being wet, closing the minute spaces between them making the tube practically water tight. This type of hose tends to deteriorate rapidly if not thoroughly dried after use or if installed where it will be exposed to dampness or the weather. It is not ordinarily built to withstand frequent service or for use where the fabric will be subjected to chafing from rough or sharp surfaces.

19. Seepage of water through an unlined linen hose is observed when the water is first turned on.
    From the above paragraph, we may conclude that the seepage

    A. indicates that the hose is defective
    B. does not indicate that the hose is defective provided that the seepage is proportionate to the water pressure
    C. does not indicate that the hose is defective provided that the seepage is greatly reduced when the hose becomes thoroughly wet
    D. does not indicate that the hose is defective provided that the seepage takes place only at the surface of the hose

20. Unlined linen hose is MOST suitable for use

   A. as a garden hose
   B. on fire department apparatus
   C. as emergency fire equipment in buildings
   D. in fire department training schools

21. The use of unlined linen hose would be LEAST appropriate in a(n)

   A. outdoor lumber yard
   B. non-fireproof office building
   C. department store
   D. cosmetic manufacturing plant

Questions 22-25.

DIRECTIONS: Questions 22 through 25 are to be answered SOLELY on the basis of the following paragraph.

The velocity of moving water droplets decreases because of aerodynamic drag forces and gravitational effects. In the case of droplets of the sizes more favorable for fire extinguishment, these aerodynamic drag forces, opposing the motion of the droplets, are proportional to the square of the diameters of the droplets and to the square of their velocity. If the initial velocity of the droplets leaving the spray nozzles is resolved into a horizontal and vertical component, the aerodynamic drag affects the horizontal component, and both the aerodynamic drag and gravitation affect the vertical component. In still air, the horizontal velocity of a moving droplet approaches zero. The vertical velocity of the droplet approaches the terminal velocity of a free falling body, which is attained when the aerodynamic drag forces are in equilibrium with the weight of the droplet. The terminal velocity represents the lower limit of the relative velocity of water drops in air. From the standpoint of fire fighting, the absolute velocity of the moving drops is also important, since the horizontal component of the absolute velocity must be sufficient for the droplets to reach the heated area surrounding the fire, and to penetrate the updraft to the seat of the fire.

22. The one of the following forces which would contribute MOST to *aerodynamic drag forces*, as that term is used in the above paragraph, is

   A. friction   B. gravity   C. inertia   D. momentum

23. Assume that water droplets in one stream have four times the diameter and the same initial velocity as droplets in a second stream.
   From the above paragraph, we may conclude that the aerodynamic drag forces on the first stream, compared to the second, initially are _____ as much.

   A. twice   B. four times
   C. eight times   D. sixteen times

24. The horizontal velocity of a moving droplet approaches zero when the

   A. horizontal velocity approaches the terminal velocity of a free falling body
   B. square of the diameter of the droplet is proportional to the square of the velocity of the droplet
   C. vertical velocity is in equilibrium with the aerodynamic drag forces
   D. maximum horizontal reach of the stream is obtained

25. The relative velocity of water droplets is equal to the absolute velocity when
    A. aerodynamic drag forces are in equilibrium with the weight of the droplets
    B. the square of the diameter of the droplets is proportional to the square of the velocity
    C. the air through which the droplets pass is still
    D. the aerodynamic drag forces equal the gravitational effects on the droplets

25.____

KEY (CORRECT ANSWERS)

1.	B	11.	C
2.	B	12.	D
3.	B	13.	C
4.	C	14.	A
5.	C	15.	A
6.	A	16.	A
7.	B	17.	C
8.	B	18.	B
9.	A	19.	C
10.	D	20.	C

21.	A
22.	A
23.	D
24.	D
25.	C

TEST 2

Questions 1-4.

DIRECTIONS: Questions 1 through 4 are to be answered SOLELY on the basis of the following paragraph.

During fire operations, all members shall be constantly alert to possibility of the crime of arson. In the event conditions indicate this possibility, the officer in command shall promptly notify the Fire Marshal. Unauthorized persons shall be prohibited from entering premises and actions of those authorized carefully noted. Members shall refrain from discussion of the fire and prevent disturbance of essential evidence. If necessary, the officer in command shall detail one or more members at location with information for the Fire Marshal upon his arrival.

1. From the above paragraph, it may be inferred that the reason for prohibiting unauthorized persons from entering the fire premises when arson is suspected is to prevent such persons from

    A. endangering themselves in the fire
    B. interfering with the firemen fighting the fire
    C. disturbing any evidence of arson
    D. committing acts of arson

2. The one of the following titles which BEST describes the subject matter of the above paragraph is

    A. TECHNIQUES OF ARSON DETECTION
    B. THE ROLE OF THE FIRE MARSHAL IN ARSON CASES
    C. FIRE SCENE PROCEDURES IN CASES OF SUSPECTED ARSON
    D. EVIDENCE IN ARSON INVESTIGATIONS

3. The one of the following statements that is MOST correct and complete is that the responsibility for detecting signs of arson at a fire belongs to the

    A. Fire Marshal
    B. Fire Marshal and officer in command
    C. Fire Marshal, officer in command, and any members detailed at location with information for the Fire Marshal
    D. members present at the scene of the fire regardless of their rank or position

4. From the above paragraph, it may be inferred that the Fire Marshal USUALLY arrives at the scene of a fire

    A. before the fire companies
    B. simultaneously with the fire companies
    C. immediately after the fire companies
    D. some time after the fire companies

Questions 5-8.

DIRECTIONS: Questions 5 through 8 are to be answered SOLELY on the basis of the following paragraph.

FIRES

The four types of fires are called Class A, Class B, Class C, and Class D. Examples of Class A fires are paper, cloth, or wood fires. The types of extinguishers used on Class A fires are foam, soda acid, or water. Class B fires are those in burning liquids. They require a smothering action for extinguishment. Carbon dioxide, dry chemical, vaporizing liquid, or foam are the types of extinguishers that are used on burning liquids. Electrical fires, such as in motors and switches, are Class C fires. A non-conducting extinguishing agent must be used for this kind of fire. Therefore, carbon dioxide, dry chemical, or vaporizing liquid extinguishers are used. Fires in motor vehicles are Class D fires; and carbon dioxide, dry chemical, or vaporizing liquid extinguishers should be used on them.

5. According to the information in the above paragraph, a fire in a can full of gasoline would be a Class _____ fire.

   A. D   B. C   C. B   D. A

6. In the above paragraph, the extinguishers recommended are entirely the same for Class _____ and Class _____ fires.

   A. B; D   B. C; D   C. B; C   D. A; B

7. According to the information in the above paragraph, a water extinguisher would MOST likely be suitable for use on which one of the following fires? A(n)

   A. fire in a truck engine
   B. fire in an electrical switch
   C. oil fire
   D. lumber fire

8. According to the information in the above paragraph, dry chemical

   A. should NOT be used on a burning liquid fire
   B. is a conducting extinguishing agent
   C. should NOT be used on a fire in a car
   D. smothers fires to put them out

Questions 9-10.

DIRECTIONS: Questions 9 and 10 are to be answered SOLELY on the basis of the following passage.

One of the greatest hazards to an industrial plant is fire. Consequently, a rigid system should be set up for periodic inspection of all types of fire protective equipment. Such inspections should include water tanks, sprinkler systems, standpipes, hose, fire plugs, extinguishers, and all other equipment used for fire protection. The schedule of inspections should be closely followed and an *accurate* record kept of each piece of equipment inspected and tested.

Along with this scheduled inspection, a careful survey should be made of new equipment needed. Recommendations should be made for replacement of defective and obsolete equipment, as well as the purchase of any additional equipment. As new processes and products are added to the manufacturing system, new fire hazards may be introduced that require individual treatment and possible special extinguishing devices. Plant inspection personnel should be sure to follow through.

Surveys should also include all means of egress from the building. Exits, stairs, fire towers, fire escapes, halls, fire alarm systems, emergency lighting systems, and places seldom used should be thoroughly inspected to determine their adequacy and readiness for emergency use.

9. Of the following titles, the one that BEST fits the above passage is

   A. NEW, USED, AND OLD FIRE PROTECTION EQUIPMENT
   B. MAINTENANCE OF FIRE PROTECTION EQUIPMENT
   C. INSPECTION OF FIRE PROTECTION EQUIPMENT
   D. OVERHAUL OF WORN OUT FIRE FIGHTING EQUIPMENT

10. As used in the above passage, the word *accurate* means

    A. exact   B. approximate   C. close   D. vague

Questions 11-15.

DIRECTIONS: Questions 11 through 15 are to be answered SOLELY on the basis of the following passage.

The sizes of living rooms shall meet the following requirements:

   a. In each apartment, there shall be at least one living room containing at least 120 square feet of clear floor area, and every other living room except a kitchen shall contain at least 70 square feet of clear floor area.
   b. Every living room which contains less than 80 square feet of clear floor area or which is located in the cellar or basement shall be at least 9 feet high and every other living room 8 feet high.

Apartments containing three or more rooms may have dining bays, which shall not exceed 55 square feet in floor surface area and shall not be deemed separate rooms or subject to the requirements for separate rooms. Every such dining bay shall be provided with at least one window containing an area at least one-eighth of the floor surface area of such dining bay.

11. The MINIMUM volume of a living room, other than a kitchen, which meets the minimum requirements of the above paragraph is one that measures _____ cubic feet.

    A. 70   B. 80   C. 630   D. 640

12. A builder proposes to construct an apartment house containing an apartment consisting of a kitchen which measures 10 feet by 6 feet, a room 12 feet by 12 feet, and one 11 feet by 7 feet.
    This apartment

    A. does not comply with the requirements of the above paragraph
    B. complies with the requirements of the above paragraph provided that it is not located in the cellar or basement

C. complies with the requirements of the above paragraph provided that the height of the smaller rooms is at least 9 feet
D. may or may not comply with the requirements of the above paragraph, depending upon the clear floor area of the kitchen

13. The one of the following definitions of the term *living room* which is MOST in accord with its meaning in the above paragraph is

    A. a sitting room or parlor
    B. the largest room in an apartment
    C. a room used for living purposes
    D. any room in an apartment containing 120 square feet of clear floor Area

14. Assume that one room in a four-room apartment measures 20 feet by 10 feet and contains a dining bay 8 feet by 6 feet. According to the above passage, the dining bay MUST be provided with a window measuring AT LEAST _____ square feet.

    A. 6   B. 7   C. 25   D. 55

15. Kitchens, according to the above passage, are

    A. not considered *living rooms*
    B. considered *living rooms* and must, therefore, meet the height and area requirements of the paragraph
    C. considered *living rooms* but they need not meet either the height or area requirements of the paragraph
    D. considered *living rooms* but they need meet only the height requirements, not the area requirements, of the paragraph

Questions 16-20.

DIRECTIONS: Questions 16 through 20 are to be answered SOLELY on the basis of the following paragraph.

Cotton fabrics treated with the XYZ Process have features which make them far superior to any previously known flame-retardant-treated cotton fabrics. XYZ are glow resistant; when exposed to flames or intense heat form tough, pliable, and protective chars; are inert physiologically to persons handling or exposed to the fabric; are only slightly heavier than untreated fabrics; and are susceptible to further wet and dry finishing treatments. In addition, the treated fabrics exhibit little or no adverse change in feel, texture, and appearance, and are shrink-, rot-, and mildew-resistant. The treatment reduces strength only slightly. Finished fabrics have *easy care* properties in that they are wrinkle-resistant and dry rapidly.

16. It is MOST accurate to state that the author, in the above paragraph, presents

    A. facts but reaches no conclusion concerning the value of the process
    B. his conclusion concerning the value of the process and facts to support his conclusion
    C. his conclusion concerning the value of the process unsupported by facts
    D. neither facts nor conclusions, but merely describes the process

17. The one of the following articles for which the XYZ Process would be MOST suitable is   17._____

   A. nylon stockings
   B. woolen shirt
   C. silk tie
   D. cotton bedsheet

18. The one of the following aspects of the XYZ Process which is NOT discussed in the above paragraph is its effects on   18._____

   A. costs
   B. washability
   C. wearability
   D. the human body

19. The MAIN reason for treating a fabric with the XYZ Process is to   19._____

   A. prepare the fabric for other wet and dry finishing treatments
   B. render it shrink-, rot-, and mildew-resistant
   C. increase its weight and strength
   D. reduce the chance that it will catch fire

20. The one of the following which would be considered a MINOR drawback of the XYZ Process is that it   20._____

   A. forms chars when exposed to flame
   B. makes fabrics mildew-resistant
   C. adds to the weight of fabrics
   D. is compatible with other finishing treatments

Questions 21-25.

DIRECTIONS: Questions 21 through 25 are to be answered SOLELY on the basis of the following paragraph.

In order to help prevent the spread of fire, it is necessary to understand the means by which heat is transmitted. Heat is transmitted through solids by a method called *conduction*. Materials vary greatly in their ability to transmit heat. Metals are good conductors of heat. On the other hand, wood, glass, pottery, asbestos, and many like substances are very poor conductors of heat and are termed insulators. It should be remembered, however, that there are no perfect insulators of heat. All will conduct heat to some extent; and if the heat continues long enough, it will be transmitted through the solid. The hazard of heat transmission is illustrated by the fact that a fire on one side of a metal wall could start a fire on the other side if combustibles were close to the wall.

21. Of the following, the BEST material to use for the handle of a metal pan to guard against heat is   21._____

   A. copper   B. iron   C. wood   D. steel

22. According to the above paragraph, *conduction* applies to the traveling of heat through a   22._____

   A. solid
   B. liquid
   C. slow-moving fluid
   D. gas

23. According to the information in the above paragraph, when storing combustible materials in a room with metal walls, it is BEST to 23.____

    A. keep the combustibles close together
    B. keep the combustibles away from the metal walls
    C. put the non-metals nearest the metal walls
    D. separate metal materials from non-metal materials

24. Based on the information in the above paragraph, which one of the following objects is the BEST conductor of heat? 24.____

    A. Pottery
    B. An oak desk
    C. A glass jar
    D. A silver spoon

25. Of the following, the title which BEST describes what the above paragraph is about is 25.____

    A. USES OF CONDUCTORS AND INSULATORS
    B. THE REASONS WHY FIRE SPREADS
    C. HEAT TRANSMISSION AND FIRES
    D. THE HAZARDS OF POOR CONDUCTION

KEY (CORRECT ANSWERS)

1.	C	11.	C
2.	C	12.	C
3.	D	13.	C
4.	D	14.	A
5.	C	15.	D
6.	B	16.	B
7.	D	17.	D
8.	D	18.	A
9.	C	19.	D
10.	A	20.	C

21. C
22. A
23. B
24. D
25. C

PREPARING WRITTEN MATERIAL

PARAGRAPH REARRANGEMENT
COMMENTARY

The sentences that follow are in scrambled order. You are to rearrange them in proper order and indicate the letter choice containing the correct answer at the space at the right.

Each group of sentences in this section is actually a paragraph presented in scrambled order. Each sentence in the group has a place in that paragraph; no sentence is to be left out. You are to read each group of sentences and decide upon the best order in which to put the sentences so as to form a well-organized paragraph.

The questions in this section measure the ability to solve a problem when all the facts relevant to its solution are not given.

More specifically, certain positions of responsibility and authority require the employee to discover connection between events sometimes, apparently, unrelated. In order to do this, the employee will find it necessary to correctly infer that unspecified events have probably occurred or are likely to occur. This ability becomes especially important when action must be taken on incomplete information.

Accordingly, these questions require competitors to choose among several suggested alternatives, each of which presents a different sequential arrangement of the events. Competitors must choose the MOST logical of the suggested sequences.

In order to do so, they may be required to draw on general knowledge to infer missing concepts or events that are essential to sequencing the given events. Competitors should be careful to infer only what is essential to the sequence. The plausibility of the wrong alternatives will always require the inclusion of unlikely events or of additional chains of events which are NOT essential to sequencing the given events.

It's very important to remember that you are looking for the best of the four possible choices, and that the best choice of all may not even be one of the answers you're given to choose from.

There is no one right way to solve these problems. Many people have found it helpful to first write out the order of the sentences, as they would have arranged them, on their scrap paper before looking at the possible answers. If their optimum answer is there, this can save them some time. If it isn't, this method can still give insight into solving the problem. Others find it most helpful to just go through each of the possible choices, contrasting each as they go along. You should use whatever method feels comfortable and works for you.

While most of these types of questions are not that difficult, we've added a higher percentage of the difficult type, just to give you more practice. Usually there are only one or two questions on this section that contain such subtle distinctions that you're unable to answer confidently. And you then may find yourself stuck deciding between two possible choices, neither of which you're sure about.

EXAMINATION SECTION
TEST 1

DIRECTIONS: The sentences that follow are in scrambled order. You are to rearrange them in proper order and indicate the letter choice containing the CORRECT answer. *PRINT THE LETTER OF THE CORRECT ANSWER IN THE SPACE AT THE RIGHT.*

1. Fire Marshal Adams has arrested a man for pulling a false alarm. He has recorded the following items of information about the incident in his notebook for use in his subsequent report:
    I. I was on surveillance at a frequently pulled false alarm box located at Edison Street and Harvard Road.
    II. At 1605 hours, I observed the white male, with long brown hair and a mustache, wearing black pants and a red shirt, pull the fire alarm box.
    III. I interviewed the officer of the first due ladder company, Lt. Morgan - L-37, who informed me that a search of the area disclosed no cause for an alarm to be transmitted.
    IV. A man wearing a red shirt, black pants, with long brown hair and a mustache came out of Ryan's Pub, located at Edison Street and Harvard Road, and walked directly to the alarm box.
    V. I stopped the man about five blocks away at 33rd Street and Harvard Road and asked him why he pulled the fire alarm box, and he replied, *Because I felt like it.*

   The MOST logical order for the above sentences to appear in the report is

   A. I, IV, II, III, V
   B. I, II, III, IV, V
   C. I, IV, III, II, V
   D. I, IV, V, II, III

   1.____

2. A fire marshal is preparing a report regarding Tom Jones, who was a witness to an arson fire at his apartment building. Following are five sentences which will be included in the report:
    I. On July 16, I responded to the fire building, address 2020 Elm Street, to interview Tom Jones.
    II. Tom Jones described the *super* (name unknown) as a middle-aged male with beard, six feet tall, wearing a blue jumpsuit.
    III. Tom Jones stated that he saw the *super* of the building next door set the fire.
    IV. After being advised of his constitutional rights at the 44th Precinct detective's squad room, the *super* confessed.
    V. I interviewed the *super* and took him to the precinct for further investigation.

   The MOST logical order for the above sentences to appear in the report is

   A. I, II, III, V, IV
   B. I, II, III, IV, V
   C. I, III, II, IV, V
   D. I, III, II, V, IV

   2.

117

3. A fire marshal is preparing a report on a shooting incident which will include the following five sentences:
    I. I ran around the corner and observed a man pointing a gun at another man.
    II. I informed the man I was a police officer and that he should drop his gun.
    III. I was on the corner of 4th Avenue and 43rd Street when I heard a gunshot coming from around the corner.
    IV. The man turned around and pointed his gun at me.
    V. I fired once, shooting him in the chest and causing him to fall to the ground.
The MOST logical order for the above sentences to appear in the report is

   A. I, III, IV, II, V
   B. IV, V, II, I, III
   C. III, I, II, IV, V
   D. III, I, V, II, IV

4. Fire Marshal Smith is writing a report. The report will include the following five sentences:
    I. I asked the woman for a description of the man and his location in the building.
    II. When I said, *Don't move, Five Marshal,* the man dropped the can containing a flammable liquid.
    III. I transmitted on my handie-talkie for fire companies to respond.
    IV. A woman approached our car and said there was a man pouring a liquid, which she thought to be gasoline, on a staircase at 123 East Street.
    V. Upon entering that location, I observed a man spilling a liquid on the floor.
The MOST logical order for the above sentences to appear on the interview sheet is

   A. IV, I, V, II, III
   B. I, IV, III, V, II
   C. V, II, IV, I, III
   D. IV, III, I, V, II

5. Fire Marshal Fox is completing an interview report for a fire in the kitchen of an apartment at 1700 Clayton Road. The following five sentences will be included in the interview report:
    I. This is the first fire in which Mrs. Brown has ever been involved.
    II. A neighbor smelled the food burning and called the Fire Department.
    III. Mrs. Brown has been a tenant in Apt. 4C for 7 years.
    IV. Mrs. Brown was very tired and laid down to rest and fell asleep.
    V. Mrs. Brown was cooking beef stew in the kitchen after coming home from work.
The MOST logical order for the above sentences to appear in the report is

   A. II, III, I, IV, V
   B. III, V, IV, II, I
   C. I, III, II, V, IV
   D. III, V, I, IV, II

6. A fire marshal is completing a report of an arson fire. The report will contain the following five statements made by a witness:
    I. I heard the sound of breaking glass; and when I looked out my window, I saw orange flames coming from the building across the street.
    II. I saw two young men on bicycles rapidly riding away, one with long blond hair, the other had long brown hair.
    III. He made a threat to get even when he was being evicted.
    IV. The young man with long blond hair was evicted from the fire building last week.
    V. The two young men rode in the direction of Flowers Avenue.
The MOST logical order for the above statements to appear in the report is

A. I, II, V, IV, III B. I, II, IV, V, III
C. III, I, V, II, IV D. III, I, II, IV, V

7. A fire marshal is preparing a report regarding an eleven-year-old who was burned in a fire at the Midtown School for Boys. The report will include the following five sentences:
    I. The child described the fire-setter as a male with glasses, five feet tall, wearing a blue uniform.
    II. On December 12, I responded to Hill Top Hospital to interview a child who was burned in a fire at the Midtown School for Boys.
    III. The male perpetrator made a full confession in front of the Assistant District Attorney at the precinct.
    IV. I responded to the school, after interviewing the boy, and found a security guard who fit the description.
    V. I interviewed the security guard and took him to the precinct for further questioning.

   The MOST logical order for the above sentences to appear in the fire report is

   A. I, IV, V, II, III B. IV, III, II, I, V
   C. II, I, IV, V, III D. II, IV, I, V, III

8. A fire marshal is preparing a report concerning a fire in an auto body shop. The report will contain the following five sentences:
    I. The shop owner stated that he argued with a customer about the cost of a repair job.
    II. The shop owner will be the complainant in the arson case.
    III. While on surveillance, my partner and I saw the fire and called it in over the Department radio.
    IV. The customer paid the bill and left saying, *I'll fix you for charging so much.*
    V. According to witnesses, the customer returned to the shop and threw a Molotov cocktail on the floor.

   The MOST logical order for the above sentences to appear in the report is

   A. I, IV, V, II, III B. III, I, IV, V, II
   C. V, I, IV, III, II D. III, V, I, IV, II

9. Security Officer Mace is completing an entry in her memo-book. The entry has the following five sentences:
    I. I observed the defendant removing a radio from a facility vehicle.
    II. I placed the defendant under arrest and escorted him to the patrolroom.
    III. I was patrolling the facility parking lot.
    IV. I asked the defendant to show identification. V. I determined that the defendant was not authorized to remove the radio.

   The MOST logical order for these sentences to be entered in Officer Mace's memo-book is

   A. I, III, II, IV, V B. II, V, IV, I, III
   C. III, I, IV, V, II D. IV, V, II, I, III

10. Security Officer Riley is completing an entry in his memo-book. The entry has the following five sentences:
    I. Anna Jones admitted that she stole Mary Green's wallet.
    II. I approached the women and asked them who they were and why they were arguing.
    III. I arrested Anna Jones for stealing Mary Green's wallet.
    IV. They identified themselves and Mary Green accused Anna Jones of stealing her wallet.
    V. I was in the lobby area when I observed two women arguing about a wallet.

    The MOST logical order for these sentences to be entered in Officer Riley's memo-book is

    A. II, IV, I, III, V B. III, I, IV, V, II
    C. IV, I, V, II, III D. V, II, IV, I, III

11. Assume that Security Officer John Ryan is completing an entry in his memobook. The entry has the following five sentences:
    I. I then cleared the immediate area of visitors and staff.
    II. I noticed smoke coming from a broom closet outside Room A71.
    III. Sergeant Mueller arrived with other officers to assist in clearing the area.
    IV. Upon investigation, I determined the smoke was due to burning material in the broom closet.
    V. I pulled the corridor fire alarm and notified Sergeant Mueller of the fire.

    The MOST logical order for these sentences to be entered in Officer Ryan's memo-book is

    A. II, III, IV, V, I B. II, IV, V, I, III
    C. IV, I, II, III, V D. V, III, II, I, IV

12. Security Officer Hernandez is completing an entry in his memobook. The entry has the following five sentences:
    I. I asked him to leave the premises immediately.
    II. A visitor complained that there was a strange man loitering in Clinic B hallway.
    III. I went to investigate and saw a man dressed in rags sitting on the floor of the hallway.
    IV. As he walked out, he started yelling that he had no place to go.
    V. I asked to see identification, but he said that he did not have any.

    The MOST logical order for these sentences to be entered in Officer Hernandez's memobook is

    A. II, III, V, I, IV B. III, I, II, IV, V
    C. IV, I, V, II, III D. III, I, V, II, IV

13. Officer Hogan is completing an entry in his memobook. The entry has the following five sentences:
    I. When the fighting had stopped, I transmitted a message requesting medical assistance for Mr. Perkins.
    II. Special Officer Manning assisted me in stopping the fight.
    III. When I arrived at the scene, I saw a client, Adam Finley, strike a facility employee, Peter Perkins.
    IV. As I attempted to break up the fight, Special Officer Manning came on the scene.
    V. I received a radio message from Sergeant Valez to investigate a possible fight in progress in the waiting room.

    The MOST logical order for these sentences to be entered in Officer Hogan's memobook is

    A. II, I, IV, V, III
    B. III, V, II, IV, I
    C. IV, V, III, I, II
    D. V, III, IV, II, I

14. Police Officer White is preparing a crime report concerning the burglary of Mr. Smith's home. The report will contain the following five sentences:
    I. Upon entering the house, Mr. Smith noticed that the mortgage money, which had been left on the kitchen table, had been taken.
    II. An investigation by the reporting Officer determined that the burglar had left the house through the first floor rear door.
    III. Further investigation revealed that there were no witnesses to the burglary.
    IV. In addition, several pieces of jewelry were missing from a first floor bedroom.
    V. After arriving at home, Mr. Smith discovered that someone had broken into the house by jimmying the front door.

    The MOST logical order for the above sentences to appear in the report is

    A. V, IV, II, III, I
    B. V, I, III, IV, II
    C. V, I, IV, II, III
    D. V, IV, II, I, III

15. Police Officer Jenner responds to the scene of a burglary at 2106 La Vista Boulevard. He is approached by an elderly man named Richard Jenkins, whose account of the incident includes the following five sentences:
    I. I saw that the lock on my apartment door had been smashed and the door was open.
    II. My apartment was a shambles; my belongings were everywhere and my television set was missing.
    III. As I walked down the hallway toward the bedroom, I heard someone opening a window.
    IV. I left work at 5:30 P.M. and took the bus home.
    V. At that time, I called the police.

    The MOST logical order for the above sentences to appear in the report is

    A. I, V, IV, II, III
    B. IV, I, II, III, V
    C. I, V, II, III, IV
    D. IV, III, II, V, I

16. Police Officer LaJolla is writing an Incident Report in which back-up assistance was required. The report will contain the following five sentences:
    I. The radio dispatcher asked what my location was and he then dispatched patrol cars for back-up assistance.
    II. At approximately 9:30 P.M., while I was walking my assigned footpost, a gunman fired three shots at me.
    III. I quickly turned around and saw a White male, approximately 5'10", with black hair, wearing blue jeans, a yellow T-shirt, and white sneakers, running across the avenue carrying a handgun.
    IV. When the back-up officers arrived, we searched the area but could not find the suspect.
    V. I advised the radio dispatcher that a gunman had just fired a gun at me, and then I gave the dispatcher a description of the man.

    The MOST logical order for the above sentences to appear in the report is

    A. III, V, II, IV, I
    B. II, III, V, I, IV
    C. III, II, IV, I, V
    D. II, V, I, III, IV

17. Police Officer Engle is completing a Complaint Report of a burglary which occurred at Monty's Bar. The following five sentences will be included in the Complaint Report:
    I. The owner said that approximately $600 was taken, along with eight bottles of expensive brandy.
    II. The burglar apparently gained entry to the bar through the window and exited through the front door.
    III. When Mr. Barrett returned to reopen the bar at 1:00 P.M., he found the front door open and items thrown all over the bar.
    IV. Mr. Barrett, the owner of Monty's Bar, said he closed the bar at 4:00 M. and locked all the doors.
    V. After interviewing the owner, I conducted a search of the bar and found that a window in the back of the bar was broken.

    The MOST logical order for the above sentences to appear in the report is

    A. II, IV, III, V, I
    B. IV, III, I, V, II
    C. IV, II, III, I, V
    D. II, V, IV, III, I

18. Police Officer Revson is writing a report concerning a vehicle pursuit. His report will include the following five sentences:
    I. I followed the vehicle for several blocks and then motioned to the driver to pull the car over to the curb and stop.
    II. I informed the radio dispatcher that I was in a high-speed pursuit.
    III. When the driver ignored me, I turned on my siren and the driver increased his speed.
    IV. The vehicle hit a tree, and I was able to arrest the driver.
    V. While on patrol in Car #4135, I observed a motorist driving suspiciously.

    The MOST logical order for the above sentences to appear in the report is

    A. V, I, III, II, IV
    B. II, V, III, I, IV
    C. V, I, II, IV, III
    D. II, I, V, IV, III

19. Crime Reports are completed by Police Officers. One section of a report contains the following five sentences:
    I. The man, seeing that the woman had the watch, pushed Mr. Lugano to the ground.
    II. Frank Lugano was walking into the Flame Diner on Queens Boulevard when he was jostled by a man in front of him.
    III. A few minutes later, Mr. Lugano told a police officer on foot patrol about a man and a woman taking his watch.
    IV. As soon as he was jostled, a woman reached toward Mr. Lugano's wrist and removed his expensive watch.
    V. The man and woman, after taking Mr. Lugano's watch, ran around the corner.

    The MOST logical order for the above sentences to appear in the report is

    A. II, IV, I, III, V
    B. II, IV, I, V, III
    C. IV, I, III, II, V
    D. IV, II, I, V, III

20. Detective Adams completed a Crime Report which includes the following five sentences:
    I. I arrived at the scene of the crime at 10:20 A.M. and began to question Mr. Sands about the security devices he had installed.
    II. Several clearly identifiable fingerprints were found.
    III. A Fingerprint Unit specialist arrived at the scene and immediately began to dust for fingerprints.
    IV. After questioning Mr. Sands, I called the Fingerprint Unit.
    V. On Friday morning at 10 A.M., Mr. Sands, the owner of the High Fashion Fur Store on Fifth Avenue, called the precinct to report that his safe had been broken into.

    The MOST logical order for the above sentences to appear in the Crime Report is

    A. I, V, IV, III, II
    B. I, V, III, IV, II
    C. V, I, IV, II, III
    D. V, I, IV, III, II

KEY (CORRECT ANSWERS)

1. A
2. D
3. C
4. A
5. B
6. A
7. C
8. B
9. C
10. D
11. B
12. A
13. D
14. C
15. B
16. B
17. B
18. A
19. B
20. D

TEST 2

DIRECTIONS: The sentences that follow are in scrambled order. You are to rearrange them in proper order and indicate the letter choice containing the CORRECT answer. *PRINT THE LETTER OF THE CORRECT ANSWER IN THE SPACE AT THE RIGHT.*

1. Police Officer Ling is preparing a Complaint Report of a missing person. His report will contain the following five sentences: 1.____
    I. I was greeted by Mrs. Miah Ali, who stated her daughter Lisa, age 17, did not return from school.
    II. I questioned Mrs. Ali as to what time her daughter left for school and what type of clothing she was wearing.
    III. I notified the Patrol Sergeant, searched the building and area, and prepared a Missing Person Complaint Report.
    IV. I received a call from the radio dispatcher to respond to 9 Maple Street, Apartment 1H, on a missing person complaint.
    V. Mrs. Ali informed me that Lisa was wearing a grey suit and black shoes, and departed for school at 7:30 A.M.

    The MOST logical order for the above sentences to appear in the report is

    A. IV, I, V, II, III   B. I, IV, V, III, II
    C. IV, I, II, V, III   D. III, I, IV, II, V

2. Police Officer Dunn is preparing a Complaint Report which will include the following five sentences: 2.____
    I.   Mrs. Field screamed and fought with the man.
    II. A man wearing a blue ski mask grabbed Mrs. Field's purse.
    III. Mrs. Field was shopping on 34th Street and Broadway at 1 o'clock in the afternoon.
    IV. The man then ran around the corner.
    V.   The man was white, five feet six inches tall with a medium build.

    The MOST logical order for the above sentences to appear in the report is

    A. I, V, II, IV, III   B. III, II, I, IV, V
    C. III, IV, V, I, II   D. V, IV, III, I, II

3. Police Officer Davis is preparing a written report concerning child abuse. The report will include the following five sentences: 3.____
    I.   I responded to the scene and was met by an adult and a child who was approximately four years old.
    II. I was notified by an unidentified pedestrian of a possible case of child abuse at 325 Belair Terrace.
    III. The adult told me that the child fell and that the police were not needed.
    IV. I felt that this might be a case of child abuse, and I requested that a Sergeant respond to the scene.
    V.   The child was bleeding from the head and had several bruises on the face.

    The MOST logical order for the above sentences to appear in the report is

    A. II, I, V, III, IV   B. I, II, IV, III, V
    C. I, III, IV, II, V   D. II, IV, I, V, III

4. The following five sentences will be part of a memobook entry concerning found property:

   I. Mr. Gustav said that while cleaning the lobby he found six credit cards and a passport.
   II. The credit cards and passport were issued to Manuel Gomez.
   III. I went to the precinct to give the property to the Desk Officer.
   IV. I prepared a receipt listing the property, gave the receipt to Mr. Gustav, and had him sign my memobook.
   V. While on foot patrol, I was approached by Mr. Gustav, the superintendent of 50-12 Maiden Parkway.

   The MOST logical order for the above sentences to appear in the memobook is

   A. V, I, II, IV, III
   B. I, II, IV, III, V
   C. V, I, III, IV, II
   D. I, IV, III, II, V

5. Police Officer Thomas is making a memobook entry that will include the following five sentences:

   I. My partner obtained a brief description of the suspects and the direction they were heading when they left the store.
   II. Edward Lemkin was asked to come with us to search the immediate area.
   III. I transmitted this information over the radio.
   IV. At the corner of 72nd Street and Broadway, our patrol car was stopped by Edward Lemkin, the owner of PJ Records.
   V. He told us that a group of teenagers stole some merchandise from his record store.

   The MOST logical order for the above sentences to appear in the report is

   A. V, IV, I, III, II
   B. IV, V, I, III, II
   C. V, I, III, II, IV
   D. IV, I, III, II, V

6. Police Officer Caldwell is completing a Complaint Report. The report will include the following five sentences:

   I. When I yelled, *Don't move, Police,* the taller man dropped the bat and ran.
   II. I asked the girl for a description of the two men.
   III. I called for an ambulance.
   IV. A young girl approached me and stated that a man with a baseball bat was beating another man in front of 1700 Grande Street.
   V. Upon approaching the location, I observed the taller man hitting the other man with the bat.

   The MOST logical order for the above sentences to appear in the report is

   A. IV, V, I, II, III
   B. V, IV, II, III, I
   C. V, I, III, IV, II
   D. IV, II, V, I, III

7. Police Officer Moore is writing a memobook entry concerning a summons he issued. The entry will contain the following five sentences:
   I. As I was walking down the platform, I heard music coming from a radio that a man was holding on his shoulder.
   II. I asked the man for some identification.
   III. I was walking in the subway when a passenger complained about a man playing a radio loudly at the opposite end of the station.
   IV. I then gave the man a summons for playing the radio. V. As soon as the man saw me approaching, he turned the radio off.
   The MOST logical order for the above sentences to appear in the memobook entry is

   A. III, V, II, I, IV
   B. I, II, V, IV, III
   C. III, I, V, II, IV
   D. I, V, II, IV, III

8. Police Officer Kashawahara is completing an Incident Report regarding fleeing suspects he had pursued earlier. The report will include the following five sentences:
   I. I saw two males attempting to break into a store through the front window.
   II. On Myrtle Avenue, they ran into an alley between two abandoned buildings.
   III. I yelled to them, *Hey, what are you guys doing by that window?*
   IV. At that time, I lost sight of the suspects and I returned to the station house.
   V. They started to run south on Wycoff Avenue heading towards Myrtle Avenue.
   The MOST logical order for the above sentences to appear in the report is

   A. I, V, II, IV, III
   B. III, V, II, IV, I
   C. I, III, V, II, IV
   D. III, I, V, II, IV

9. Police Officer Bloom is completing an entry in his memo-book regarding a confession made by a perpetrator. The entry will include the following five sentences:
   I. I went towards the dresser and took $400 in cash and a jewelry box with rings, watches, and other items in it.
   II. There in the bedroom, lying on the bed, a woman was sleeping.
   III. It was about 1:00 A.M. when I entered the apartment through an opened rear window.
   IV. I spun around, punched her in the face with my free hand, and then jumped out the window into the street.
   V. I walked back to the window carrying the money and the jewelry box and was about to go out when all of a sudden I heard the woman scream.
   The MOST logical order for the above sentences to appear in the memobook entry is

   A. I, III, II, V, IV
   B. I, V, IV, III, II
   C. III, II, I, V, IV
   D. III, V, IV, I, II

10. Police Officer Webster is preparing an Arrest Report which will include the following five sentences:
    I. I noticed that the robber had a knife placed at the victim's neck.
    II. I told the robber to drop the knife.
    III. While on patrol, I observed a robbery which was in progress.
    IV. I grabbed the robber, placed him in handcuffs, and took him to the precinct.
    V. The robber dropped the knife and tried to flee.
    The MOST logical order for the above sentences to appear in the report is

    A. I, II, V, IV, III
    B. III, I, II, V, IV
    C. III, II, IV, I, V
    D. I, III, IV, V, II

11. Police Officer Lee is preparing a report regarding someone who apparently attempted to commit suicide with a gun. The report will include the following five sentences:
    I. At the location, the woman pointed to the open door of Apartment 7L.
    II. I called for an ambulance to respond.
    III. The male had a gun in his hand and a large head wound.
    IV. A call was received from the radio dispatcher regarding a woman who heard a gunshot at 936 45th Avenue.
    V. Upon entering Apartment 7L, I saw the body of a male on the kitchen floor.
    The MOST logical order for the above sentences to appear in the report is

    A. IV, I, V, III, II
    B. I, III, V, IV, II
    C. I, V, III, II, IV
    D. IV, V, III, II, I

11.____

12. Police Officer Modrak is completing a memobook entry which will include the following five sentences:
    I. The victim, a male in his thirties, told me that the robbery occurred a few minutes ago.
    II. My partner and I jumped out of the patrol car and arrested the suspect.
    III. We responded to an armed robbery in progress at Billings Avenue and 59th Street.
    IV. On Chester Avenue and 68th Street, the victim spotted and identified the suspect.
    V. I told the victim to get into the patrol car and that we would drive him around the area.
    The MOST logical order for the above sentences to appear in the memobook is

    A. III, I, V, IV, II
    B. I, III, V, II, IV
    C. I, IV, III, V, II
    D. III, V, I, II, IV

12.____

13. Police Officer Rodriguez is preparing a report concerning an incident in which she used her revolver. Her report will include the following five sentences:
    I. Upon seeing my revolver, the robber dropped his gun to the ground.
    II. At about 10:55 P.M., I was informed by a passerby that several people were being robbed at gunpoint on 174th Street and Walton Avenue.
    III. I was assigned to patrol on 174th Street and Ghent Avenue during the evening shift.
    IV. I saw a man holding a gun on three people, took out my revolver, and shouted, *Police, don't move!*
    V. After calling for assistance, I went to 174th Street and Walton Avenue and took cover behind a car.
    The MOST logical order for the above sentences to appear in the report is

    A. II, III, IV, V, I
    B. IV, V, I, III, II
    C. III, II, V, IV, I
    D. II, IV, I, V, III

13.____

14. Police Officer Davis is completing an Activity Log entry which will include the following five sentences:
    I. A radio car was dispatched and the male was taken to Greenville Hospital.
    II. Several people saw him and called the police.
    III. A naked man was running down the street waving his arms above his head and screaming, *Insects are all over me!*
    IV. I arrived on the scene and requested an ambulance.
    V. The dispatcher informed me that no ambulances were available.

    The MOST logical order for the above sentences to appear in the Activity Log is

    A. III, IV, V, I, II
    B. II, III, V, I, IV
    C. III, II, IV, V, I
    D. II, IV, III, V, I

15. Police Officer Peake is completing an entry in his Activity Log. The entry contains the following five sentences:
    I. He went to his parked car only to find he was blocked in.
    II. The owner of the vehicle refused to move the van until he had finished his lunch.
    III. Approximately 30 minutes later, I arrived on the scene and ordered the owner of the van to remove the vehicle.
    IV. Mr. O'Neil had an appointment and was in a hurry to keep it.
    V. Mr. O'Neil entered a nearby delicatessen and asked if anyone in there drove a dark blue van, license plate number BUS 265.

    The MOST logical order for the above sentences to appear in the Activity Log is

    A. II, III, I, IV, V
    B. IV, I, V, II, III
    C. V, IV, I, III, II
    D. II, I, III, IV, V

16. Police Officer Harrison is preparing a report regarding a 10-year-old who was sexually abused at school. The report will include the following five sentences:
    I. The child described the perpetrator as a white male with a mustache, six feet tall, wearing a green uniform.
    II. On September 10, I responded to General Hospital to interview a child who was sexually abused.
    III. He later confessed at the station house.
    IV. After I interviewed the child, I responded to the school and found a janitor who fit the description.
    V. I interviewed the janitor and took him to the station house for further investigation.

    The MOST logical order for the above sentences to appear in the report is

    A. II, IV, I, V, III
    B. I, IV, V, II, III
    C. II, I, IV, V, III
    D. V, III, II, I, IV

17. Police Officer Madden is completing a report of a theft. The report will include the following five sentences:
    I. I followed behind the suspect for two blocks.
    II. I saw a man pass by the radio car carrying a shopping bag.
    III. I looked back in the direction he had just come from and noticed that the top of a parking meter was missing.
    IV. As he saw me, he started to walk faster, and I noticed a red piece of metal with the word *violation* drop out of the shopping bag.
    V. When I saw a parking meter in the shopping bag, I apprehended the suspect and placed him under arrest.

    The MOST logical order for the above sentences to appear in the report is

    A. I, IV, II, III, V
    B. II, I, IV, V, III
    C. II, IV, III, I, V
    D. III, II, IV, I, V

18. Police Officer McCaslin is preparing a report of disorderly conduct which will include the following five sentences:
    I. Police Officer Kenny and I were on patrol in a radio car when we received a dispatch to go to the Hard Rock Disco on Third Avenue.
    II. We arrived at the scene and found three men arguing loudly and obviously intoxicated.
    III. The dispatcher had received a call from a bartender regarding a dispute.
    IV. Two of the men left the disco shortly before we did.
    V. We calmed the men down after managing to separate them.

    The MOST logical order for the above sentences to appear in the report is

    A. I, II, V, III, IV
    B. III, I, IV, II, V
    C. II, I, III, IV, V
    D. I, III, II, V, IV

19. Police Officer Langhorne is completing a report of a murder. The report will contain the following five statements made by a witness:
    I. The noise created by the roar of a motorcycle caused me to look out of my window.
    II. I ran out of the house and realized the man was dead, which is when I called the police.
    III. I saw a man driving at high speed down the dead-end street on a motorcycle, closely followed by a green BMW.
    IV. The motorcyclist then parked the bike and approached the car, which was occupied by two males.
    V. Two shots were fired and the cyclist fell to the ground; then the car made a u-turn and sped down the street.

    The MOST logical order for the above sentences to appear in the report is

    A. I, II, IV, III, V
    B. V, II, I, IV, III
    C. I, III, IV, V, II
    D. III, IV, I, II, V

20. Police Officer Murphy is preparing a report of a person who was assaulted. The report will include the following five sentences:
    I. I responded to the scene, but Mr. Jones had already fled.
    II. She was bleeding profusely from a cut above her right eye.
    III. Mr. and Mrs. Jones apparently were fighting in the street when Mr. Jones punched his wife in the face.
    IV. I then applied pressure to the cut to control the bleeding.
    V. I called the dispatcher on the radio to send an ambulance to respond to the scene.

    The MOST logical order for the above sentences to appear in the report is

    A. III, II, IV, I, V
    B. III, I, II, IV, V
    C. I, V, II, III, IV
    D. II, V, IV, III, I

20.____

KEY (CORRECT ANSWERS)

1.	C	11.	A
2.	B	12.	A
3.	A	13.	C
4.	A	14.	C
5.	B	15.	B
6.	D	16.	C
7.	C	17.	C
8.	C	18.	D
9.	C	19.	C
10.	B	20.	B

PREPARING WRITTEN MATERIALS
EXAMINATION SECTION
TEST 1

DIRECTIONS: Each question consists of a sentence which may be classified appropriately under one of the following four categories:
- A. Incorrect because of faulty grammar or sentence structure.
- B. Incorrect because of faulty punctuation.
- C. Incorrect because of faulty spelling or capitalization.
- D. Correct

Examine each sentence carefully. Then, in the space at the right, print the capital letter preceding the option which is the BEST of the four suggested above. All incorrect sentences contain only one type of error. Consider a sentence correct if it contains none of the types of errors mentioned, although there may be other correct ways of expressing the same thought.

1. The fire apparently started in the storeroom, which is usually locked. 1.____
2. On approaching the victim two bruises were noticed by this officer. 2.____
3. The officer, who was there examined the report with great care. 3.____
4. Each employee in the office had a separate desk. 4.____
5. The suggested procedure is similar to the one now in use. 5.____
6. No one was more pleased with the new procedure than the chauffeur. 6.____
7. He tried to pursuade her to change the procedure. 7.____
8. The total of the expenses charged to petty cash were high. 8.____
9. An understanding between him and I was finally reached. 9.____
10. It was at the supervisor's request that the clerk agreed to postpone his vacation. 10.____
11. We do not believe that it is necessary for both he and the clerk to attend the conference. 11.____
12. All employees, who display perseverance, will be given adequate recognition. 12.____
13. He regrets that some of us employees are dissatisfied with our new assignments. 13.____

14. "Do you think that the raise was merited," asked the supervisor? 14._____

15. The new manual of procedure is a valuable supplament to our rules and regulation. 15._____

16. The typist admitted that she had attempted to pursuade the other employees to assist her in her work. 16._____

17. The supervisor asked that all amendments to the regulations be handled by you and I. 17._____

18. They told both he and I that the prisoner had escaped. 18._____

19. Any superior officer, who, disregards the just complaints of his subordinates, is remiss in the performance of his duty. 19._____

20. Only those members of the national organization who resided in the Middle west attended the conference in Chicago. 20._____

21. We told him to give the investigation assignment to whoever was available. 21._____

22. Please do not disappoint and embarass us by not appearing in court. 22._____

23. Despite the efforts of the Supervising mechanic, the elevator could not be started. 23._____

24. The U.S. Weather Bureau, weather record for the accident date was checked. 24._____

KEY (CORRECT ANSWERS)

1.	D	11.	A
2.	A	12.	B
3.	B	13.	D
4.	D	14.	B
5.	D	15.	C
6.	D	16.	C
7.	C	17.	A
8.	A	18.	A
9.	A	19.	B
10.	D	20.	C

21. D
22. C
23. C
24. B

TEST 2

DIRECTIONS: Each question consists of a sentence. Some of the sentences contain errors in English grammar or usage, punctuation, spelling, or capitalization. A sentence does not contain an error simply because it could be written in a different manner. Choose answer:
- A. If the sentence contains an error in English grammar or usage.
- B. if the sentence contains an error in punctuation.
- C. If the sentence contains an error in spelling or capitalization
- D. If the sentence does not contain any errors.

1. The severity of the sentence prescribed by contemporary statutes—including both the former and the revised New York Penal Laws—do not depend on what crime was intended by the offender. 1.____

2. It is generally recognized that two defects in the early law of attempt played a part in the birth of burglary: (1) immunity from prosecution for conduct short of the last act before completion of the crime, and (2) the relatively minor penalty imposed for an attempt (it being a common law misdemeanor) vis-à-vis the completed offense. 2.____

3. The first sentence of the statute is applicable to employees who enter their place of employment, invited guests, and all other persons who have an express or implied license or privilege to enter the premises. 3.____

4. Contemporary criminal codes in the United States generally divide burglary into various degrees, differentiating the categories according to place, time and other attendent circumstances. 4.____

5. The assignment was completed in record time but the payroll for it has not yet been prepaid. 5.____

6. The operator, on the other hand, is willing to learn me how to use the mimeograph. 6.____

7. She is the prettiest of the three sisters. 7.____

8. She doesn't know; if the mail has arrived. 8.____

9. The doorknob of the office door is broke. 9.____

10. Although the department's supply of scratch pads and stationery have diminished considerably, the allotment for our division has not been reduced. 10.____

11. You have not told us whom you wish to designate as your secretary. 11.____

12. Upon reading the minutes of the last meeting, the new proposal was taken up for consideration. 12.____

13. Before beginning the discussion, we locked the door as a precautionery measure. 13.____

14. The supervisor remarked, "Only those clerks, who perform routine work, are permitted to take a rest period." 14.____

15. Not only will this duplicating machine make accurate copies, but it will also produce a quantity of work equal to fifteen transcribing typists. 15.____

16. "Mr. Jones," said the supervisor, "we regret our inability to grant you an extention of your leave of absence." 16.____

17. Although the employees find the work monotonous and fatigueing, they rarely complain. 17.____

18. We completed the tabulation of the receipts on time despite the fact that Miss Smith our fastest operator was absent for over a week. 18.____

19. The reaction of the employees who attended the meeting, as well as the reaction of those who did not attend, indicates clearly that the schedule is satisfactory to everyone concerned. 19.____

20. Of the two employees, the one in our office is the most efficient. 20.____

21. No one can apply or even understand, the new rules and regulations. 21.____

22. A large amount of supplies were stored in the empty office. 22.____

23. If an employee is occassionally asked to work overtime, he should do so willingly. 23.____

24. It is true that the new procedures are difficult to use but, we are certain that you will learn them quickly. 24.____

25. The office manager said that he did not know who would be given a large allotment under the new plan. 25.____

KEY (CORRECT ANSWERS)

1.	A	11.	D
2.	D	12.	A
3.	D	13.	C
4.	C	14.	B
5.	C	15.	A
6.	A	16.	C
7.	D	17.	C
8.	B	18.	B
9.	A	19.	D
10.	A	20.	A

21. B
22. A
23. C
24. B
25. D

TEST 3

DIRECTIONS: Each of the following sentences may be classified MOST appropriately under one of the following categories:
- A. Faulty because of incorrect grammar
- B. Faulty because of incorrect punctuation
- C. Faulty because of incorrect capitalization
- D. Correct

Examine each sentence carefully. Then, in the space at the right, print the capital letter preceding the option which is the BEST of the four suggested above. All incorrect sentence contain but one type of error. Consider a sentence correct if it contains none of the types of errors mentioned, even though there may be other correct ways of expressing the same thought.

1. The desk, as well as the chairs, were moved out of the office. 1.____

2. The clerk whose production was greatest for the month won a day's vacation as first prize. 2.____

3. Upon entering the room, the employees were found hard at work at their desks. 3.____

4. John Smith our new employee always arrives at work on time. 4.____

5. Punish whoever is guilty of stealing the money. 5.____

6. Intelligent and persistent effort lead to success no matter what the job may be. 6.____

7. The secretary asked, "can you call again at three o'clock?" 7.____

8. He told us, that if the report was not accepted at the next meeting, it would have to be rewritten. 8.____

9. He would not have sent the letter if he had known that it would cause so much excitement. 9.____

10. We all looked forward to him coming to visit us. 10.____

11. If you find that you are unable to complete the assignment please notify me as soon as possible. 11.____

12. Every girl in the office went home on time but me; there was still some work for me to finish. 12.____

13. He wanted to know who the letter was addressed to, Mr. Brown or Mr. Smith. 13.____

14. "Mr. Jones, he said, please answer this letter as soon as possible." 14.____

15. The new clerk had an unusual accent inasmuch as he was born and educated in the south. 15._____

16. Although he is younger than her, he earns a higher salary. 16._____

17. Neither of the two administrators are going to attend the conference being held in Washington, D.C. 17._____

18. Since Miss Smith and Miss Jones have more experience than us, they have been given more responsible duties. 18._____

19. Mr. Shaw the supervisor of the stock room maintains an inventory of stationery and office supplies. 19._____

20. Inasmuch as this matter affects both you and I, we should take joint action. 20._____

21. Who do you think will be able to perform this highly technical work? 21._____

22. Of the two employees, John is considered the most competent. 22._____

23. He is not coming home on tuesday; we expect him next week. 23._____

24. Stenographers, as well as typists must be able to type rapidly and accurately. 24._____

25. Having been placed in the safe we were sure that the money would not be stolen. 25._____

KEY (CORRECT ANSWERS)

1.	A		11.	B
2.	D		12.	D
3.	A		13.	A
4.	B		14.	B
5.	D		15.	C
6.	A		16.	A
7.	C		17.	A
8.	B		18.	A
9.	D		19.	B
10.	A		20.	A

21. D
22. A
23. C
24. B
25. A

TEST 4

DIRECTIONS: Each of the following sentences consist of four sentences lettered A, B, C, and D. One of the sentences in each group contains an error in grammar or punctuation. Indicate the INCORRECT sentence in each group. *PRINT THE LETTER OF THE CORRECT ANSWER IN THE SPACE AT THE RIGHT.*

1. A. Give the message to whoever is on duty.
    B. The teacher who's pupil won first prize presented the award.
    C. Between you and me, I don't expect the program to succeed.
    D. His running to catch the bus caused the accident.

    1.____

2. A. The process, which was patented only last year is already obsolete.
    B. His interest in science (which continues to the present) led him to convert his basement into a laboratory.
    C. He described the book as "verbose, repetitious, and bombastic".
    D. Our new director will need to possess three qualities: vision, patience, and fortitude.

    2.____

3. A. The length of ladder trucks varies considerably.
    B. The probationary fireman reported to the officer to who he was assigned.
    C. The lecturer emphasized the need for we firemen to be punctual.
    D. Neither the officers nor the members of the company knew about the new procedure.

    3.____

4. A. Ham and eggs is the specialty of the house.
    B. He is one of the students who are on probation.
    C. Do you think that either one of us have a chance to be nominated for president of the class?
    D. I assume that either he was to be in charge or you were.

    4.____

5. A. Its a long road that has no turn.
    B. To run is more tiring than to walk.
    C. We have been assigned three new reports: namely, the statistical summary, the narrative summary, and the budgetary summary.
    D. Had the first payment been made in January, the second would be due in April.

    5.____

6. A. Each employer has his own responsibilities.
    B. If a person speaks correctly, they make a good impression.
    C. Every one of the operators has had her vacation.
    D. Has anybody filed his report?

    6.____

7. A. The manager, with all his salesmen, was obliged to go.
    B. Who besides them is to sign the agreement?
    C. One report without the others is incomplete.
    D. Several clerks, as well as the proprietor, was injured.

    7.____

8. A. A suspension of these activities is expected.
    B. The machine is economical because first cost and upkeep are low.
    C. A knowledge of stenography and filing are required for this position.
    D. The condition in which the goods were received shows that the packing was not done properly.

9. A. There seems to be a great many reasons for disagreement.
    B. It does not seem possible that they could have failed.
    C. Have there always been too few applicants for these positions?
    D. There is no excuse for these errors.

10. A. We shall be pleased to answer your question.
    B. Shall we plan the meeting for Saturday?
    C. I will call you promptly at seven.
    D. Can I borrow your book after you have read it?

11. A. You are as capable as I.
    B. Everyone is willing to sign but him and me.
    C. As for he and his assistant, I cannot praise them too highly.
    D. Between you and me, I think he will be dismissed.

12. A. Our competitors bid above us last week.
    B. The survey which was began last year has not yet been completed.
    C. The operators had shown that they understood their instructions.
    D. We have never ridden over worse roads.

13. A. Who did they say was responsible?
    B. Whom did you suspect?
    C. Who do you suppose it was?
    D. Whom do you mean?

14. A. Of the two propositions, this is the worse.
    B. Which report do you consider the best—the one in January or the one in July?
    C. I believe this is the most practicable of the many plans submitted.
    D. He is the youngest employee in the organization.

15. A. The firm had but three orders last week.
    B. That doesn't really seem possible.
    C. After twenty years scarcely none of the old business remains.
    D. Has he done nothing about it?

KEY (CORRECT ANSWERS)

1.	B	6.	B	11.	C
2.	A	7.	D	12.	B
3.	C	8.	C	13.	A
4.	C	9.	A	14.	B
5.	A	10.	D	15.	C

THE BUILDING AND ITS MAKEUP

TABLE OF CONTENTS

	Page
BUILDING CONSTRUCTION	1
Introduction	1
General Construction Principles	1
Types of Building Construction	2
Building Materials and Contents	3
Building Code Requirements	7
Involvement of Ceilings	8
Building Elements	8
Interior Finish	9
MATERIALS	11
Introduction	11
Properties of Materials	11
Classes of Materials	12
UTILITY SYSTEMS	17
Introduction	17
Heating, Ventilation and Air Conditioning	18
Electrical	21

THE BUILDING AND ITS MAKEUP

BUILDING CONSTRUCTION

Introduction

In many cases the design, construction, and use of the building contributes to the initiation and severity of serious building fires. For these reasons, a knowledge of buildings, how they are constructed, and with what kinds of materials, is important to the fire investigator.

A knowledge and use of the correct terminology of building construction also is important in the writing of accurate reports, as well as in courtroom appearances. As an example, the investigator should know and be able to describe the similarities and the differences between spandrels, beams, and girders.

Sometimes in getting at the fire cause, it is necessary to "reconstruct" the arrangement and condition of the room or area of fire involvement to understand the development and spread of the fire. To do this "reconstruct", it is necessary to know what kinds of building materials and construction were likely to have been present prior to the fire damage. (Where there are similar rooms or areas available in the same or similar buildings, such as in hotels or garden apartments, a method to "reconstruct" is to examine undamaged units.)

General Construction Principles

The fire investigator should be familiar with the basic principles of building construction.

The initial concern of fire resistance provisions in building codes is that the building should not collapse as a result of a fire. Secondarily, the structure should limit the fire to an area of acceptable size.

Some elements of the system are more vulnerable to fire than others. When a fire occurs, the building is only as stable as the weakest (to fire) element.

All loads must be transmitted continuously to ground. This is accomplished by a multitude of structural components and connections in the structure. The importance of the connections varies. In some cases, the failure of a connection may have only a local effect. In other cases, the failure may be catastrophic in that a building collapse may occur.

Principal structural materials are wood, masonry (stone, brick, and concrete block), steel and reinforced concrete.

The principal elements of structures are walls, columns, and beams. Walls and columns carry the loads of the building down to the earth. Beams carry the loads generated on each floor of the building to the columns or walls.

Walls may be load-bearing, that is, carrying a load other than themselves, or be nonload-bearing, typically partitions and exterior veneer walls.

Columns carry vertical loads to the ground or foundation. Because columns take up space, suspension rods or cables in tension are sometimes used to "hang" certain loads in a building.

The system must, however, provide for the tensile load to be carried over into a column or wall and delivered to the earth in compression.

Floors and roofs are supported on beams and girders as well as on walls. A girder is a beam which supports other beams. Since beams must resist both tension (usually in the bottom of the beam) and compression forces (usually in the top), solid beams contain excess material. In many cases, the load can be carried on a lighter unit called a truss, which eliminates excess material. A trussconsists of a series of specially connected and designed load-carrying elements and open spaces, which makes it more vulnerable to fire and thus more likely to collapse than an equivalent solid beam.

Types of Building Construction

There are five basic construction types. Various building codes subdivide these types further (see table 1) The five types are:

Table 1 Types of Construction According to Model codes*

Construction Type	Basic Building Code, by Type (BOCA)	Standard Building Code, by Type (SBC)	Uniform Building Code, by type (UBC)	National Building Code, by Type (NBC)
Fire Resistive	1A	I	I	A
	1B	II	I	B
Noncombustiable Protected	2A		II (4 hr)	
	2B	IV (1 hr)	II (1 hr)	Protected Noncombustiable
None combustible Unprotected	2C	IV	II (N)	Unprotected Noncombustiable
Heavy Timber	3A	III	IV (HT)	Heavy Timber
Ordinary Protected	3B	V (1 hr)	III (1hr)	
Ordinary Unprotected	3C	V	III (N)	Ordinary
Wood Frame Protected	4A	VI (1hr)	V (1hr)	
Wood Frame Unprotected	4B	VI	V (N)	Wood Frame

* This Table indicates the type assigned by the respective codes to various construction types. It is not intended to indicate that different codes necessarily have identical requirements for any specific type.

Fire Resistive
Noncombustible
Heavy Timber
Ordinary Wood Frame
Wood Frame

The investigator's report should use the terminology of the appropriate local code.

Note that the commonly used word "fireproof" does not appear in the list of types, though it may appear in some codes. When designers first considered fire as a problem they believed that all fire problems would be eliminated by constructing the building of noncombustible material. Such buildings were called "fireproof" and the misnomer has persisted. Early "fireproof" buildings were found deficient when put to the test of actual fires since all noncombustible materials will lose strength at sufficiently high temperatures. As technology improved, the term "fire resistive" emerged.

Fire Resistive buildings are ones in which specimens of the major structural components have been rated by standard fire endurance tests during which collapse and passage of fire, where appropriate, were resisted for prescribed periods of time. No direct relationship should be assumed between the "time" of the controlled test and an uncontrolled hostile fire. Whereas each of the elements of the building may meet fire resistance criteria, it is most unlikely that the building as a whole was ever analyzed for the total impact of a potential fire, and "the whole may be less than the sum of the parts". Fire resistance does not guarantee life safety. Fire resistance is not necessarily related to fire loss; in fact, while achieving its designed fire resistance, the structure may be damaged severely. Fire resistive assemblies are not necessarily noncombustible. Floors and walls of wood and gypsum board are assigned fire resistance ratings by UL (Underwriters Laboratories Inc.), even though the assemblies are combustible.

Depending upon how the fire resistance is achieved, different buildings of the same fire resistance rating may exhibit different characteristics in similar fires. For instance, a fire resistive floor of reinforced concrete absorbs considerable heat. A steel joist floor and ceiling assembly, of equal fire resistance, will not absorb as much heat. This can affect the propagation of a fire, as every Btu absorbed by the structure is one less available to keep the fire growing. As a second example, a rated reinforced concrete floor may act as a very effective smoke barrier. An equally rated floor and ceiling assembly with an integral air handling system could provide a path for travel of smoke and gases. This property is not considered in the test rating.

Noncombustible buildings are ones in which the walls, partitions and structural members are of noncombustible construction not qualifying as fire resistive construction.

Heavy Timber construction buildings have masonry exterior walls and heavy timber interiors. The concept is that the heavy timber is slow to ignite and burns at a slow enough rate that collapse may be delayed. The concept fails once the fire involves the building and the fire suppression forces cannot sustain an interior attack. The massive amount of timber then simply becomes a tremendous fire load.

Ordinary Construction buildings have masonry exterior walls and lightly constructed combustible interiors. The principal benefit of the masonry walls is to reduce the conflagration potential. The interior is expected to collapse in a fire and may be required by code to be so designed, the so-called fire cuts on wood joists are an example.

Wood Frame buildings are basically of wood construction. A noncombustible veneer, such as brick, does not change the nature or classification of the building.

Building Materials and Contents

Code regulations which limit the type and size of construction are predicated on the type of building, the type of occupancy anticipated, and the anticipated level of potential fire risk.

Estimates of the potential fire risk are based to a large extent on the fire load (or fuel load). For buildings of combustible construction the basic fire load is the building itself, thus such buildings are usually limited by code in area and height. In addition, for all buildings the weight of combustible contents per unit of floor area must be considered. Fire loads are usually expressed in the term pounds (of ordinary combustibles) per square foot. All weights are commonly converted to the equivalent of ordinary combustibles such as wood which has a heat value of about 8,000 Btu/lb. For instance, plastics which have a heat value of about 16,000 Btu/lb are converted at the rate of 1 lb of plastic to 2 lb ordinary combustibles.

Typical ranges of fire loads for the more common occupancy classes are shown in table 2. However, fire loads can vary considerably according to the occupancy the specific location in the building, and, other factors.

Table 2 Typical Fire Loads

Occupancy Classification	Typical Range of Fire Loads lb/sq ft
Residential	5 to 10
Educational	5 to 10
(Library)	(10 to 40)
Institutional	3 to 10
Assembly	5 to 10
Business (office)	5 to 10
(File, Storage)	(10 to 40)
Mercantile	10 to 20
Industrial	10 to 35
Storage	10 to 100
Hazardous	*

* No typical values available. Risk based on factors other than fire load

Structural fire protection requirements in building codes are based on fire resistance or fire endurance ratings expressed in hours. The ratings are basedon fire tests performed on the structural or compartmenting (separating) building components according to the NFPA 251 (ASTM E 119) standardized test procedure, The exposure is such that a temperature of 1000°F (538°C) is reached in 5 min, 1700°F (927°C) in 1 hr, 1850°F (1010°C) in 2 hrs, 2000°F (1093°C) in 4 hrs and 2300°F (1260°C) in 8 hrs. These temperatures-vs.-time points produce a curve which is referred to as the fire endurance standard time-temperature curve. The test is conducted in a special test furnace and continued until one of several criteria of failure, as appropriate, is reached: (a) structural failure (inability to sustain the applied load), (b) integrity failure (development of a crack or opening through which flames or hot gases may pass during the fire test, or a hose stream test) or, (c) insulation failure (heat transmission sufficient to raise the temperature on the unexposed surface by 250°F (139°C) average).

Although the standard fire test curve represents only one type of fire exposure, it serves as a useful means for the comparative rating of individual columns, beams, walls, partitions, and floor and ceiling assemblies. Again, it should be stressed that although the ratings are expressed in hours, the relationship between the rating hours and hours of an actual fire assault on a building may differ.

A relationship between fire load and equivalent fire endurance period was developed many years ago based on experimental burnouts of combustibles in special masonry test buildings and is shown in table 3. Table.3 indicates that the burning of a fire load of 10 lbs of ordinary combustibles per square foot (or 80,000 Btu/sq ft) is the approximate equivalent of 1 hour of the standard fire test ASTM E 119.

If these figures are used cautiously and broadly, rather than precisely, it is possible to estimate whether, in a given fire, the fire load was grossly excessive for the fire resistance of the building. Consider a building with floors rated two-hour fire-resistive. Such a building might reasonably be expected to successfully resist a fire involving a design fire load of 160,000 Btu/sq ft average. On the other hand, an investigator may estimate that in the affected area of an actual fire, the fire load was 300,000 Btu/sq ft average. It can be reasonably concluded that the fire area was overloaded from the fire endurance point of view, even though the total structural loading may have been within permissible limits.

Table 3. Fire Load versus Equivalent Fire Endurance Period in Standard Fire Test

Fire Load 1b sq ft	Equivalent Fire Endurance Period hr
5	½
7 ½	¾
10	1
15	1 ½
20	2
30	3
40	4 ½
50	6
60	7 ½

Structural members and floors are made fire resistive in a variety of ways.
Reinforced concrete has inherent fire resistance. This inherent fire resistance can be increased to the desired level by increasing the concrete cover over the "reinforcing" steel. If the depth of the concrete cover is not as specified, early failure may result.

Steel must be protected from the harmful effects of elevated temperatures (loss of strength, elongation and heat transmission). Protection can be accomplished in several ways, including encasement, sprayed fireproofing, membrane protection or by using water- filled columns. In a particular building more than one way may be used.

Encasement. Each structural steel member is encased in an insulating cover; hollow tile, poured concrete, concrete block, wire lath and plaster or gypsum board are typically used.

Sprayed "Fireproofing". In this case structural steel members are spraye or trowele with plaster containing inorganic fibers or cement. One common material formerly used, asbestos, is held responsible for health hazards due to inhalation in many buildings. In some cases this has caused its removal, sometimes without any provision for replacing the necessary fire resistance. Sprayed "fireproofing" may be poorly done and in many cases is found to have fallen off or been removed by other building trades

Membrane Protection. Large areas, such as entire floors, are protected by a membrane,"consisting typically of a wire lath and plaster ceiling or a suspended ceiling of individual panels. The problem is that, like all membranes, a single penetration may reduce the effectiveness of the entire membrane. Wire lath and plaster membranes are designed to be permanent and generally left in place but individual acoustical tile (panel) ceilings are readily removable.

The entire floor and ceiling assembly is fire rated as a unit. The presumption is that the unit is installed the same way as the unit tested. Even if this is accomplished, the ceiling tiles may be removed for many reasons. The fact that the ceiling tiles are part of the fire resistance of the building is unknown to many building owners and operators and fire inspectors. Untested penetrations as for sound system speakers are another weakness. Any tampering with the ceiling opens the entire floor area up to attack by fire. The void space between the ceiling and the floor above represents a potential for lateral fire spread between every floor of the building. There can be a substantial fire load in the void due to plastic insulation and piping, and lightweight merchandise is sometimes found stored in the void.

In one case, fire in one occupancy entered the void and extended downward to combustible shelves and contents in the next occupancy, This was detected early enough to clearly show what had happened. Had the extension not been detected, all appearances would have been of two separate fires. In fact, the fire was incendiary and successfully prosecuted. Failure to describe the development of the fire accurately might have led to a loss of the case.

Current lists of fire rated constructions and assemblies are maintained by Underwriters Laboratories -- the American Insurance Association -- and the Factory Mutual System.

Almost any structure has some degree of fire resistance, even though it is itself combustible. Table 4 is provided to enable the investigator to develop estimated fire resistance values for some common wall and floor assemblies. It consists of two parts. In the first part values are given for some common materials used as membranes (the surface finish). The second part gives values for framing members

For example, using table 4, unprotected open web steel joists are assigned a value of 7 minutes. With 1/2" gypsum wallboard properly attached and sealed, the combination could be assigned a time of 22 minutes (7 minutes for the steel joists, 15 minutes for the gypsum wallboard).

A wood stud wall with 1/2" gypsum board on both sides could be assigned a value of 50 minutes (20 minutes for the studs plus 15 minutes for each layer of the wallboard). It should be stated here again that the times referred to are estimates of how long the structure in question would continue to meet the standards of ASTM E 119 (NFPA 251) when tested in accordance with that standard. There is no necessary relationship to elapsed time in a hostile fire.

Table 4 Time Assigned to wallboard membranes

Description of Finish		Time Assigned to Membrane in Minutes
(i)	½ in Fiberboard	5
(ii)	³/₈ in Douglas Fir Plywood Phenolic bonded	5
(iii)	½ in Douglas Fir Plywood Phenolic bonded	10
(iv)	⁵/₈ in Douglas Fir Plywood Phenolic bonded	15
(v)	³/₈ in Gypsum Wallboard	10
(vi)	½ in Gypsum Wallboard	15
(vii)	⁵/₈ in Gypsum Wallboard	30
(viii)	Double ³/₈ in gypsum Wallboard	25
(ix)	½ + ³/₈ in Gypsum Wallboard	35
(x)	Double ½ in Gypsum Wallboard	50(1)
(xi)	³/₁₆ in Asb. Cem. + in Gypsum Wallboard	40(2)
(xii)	³/₁₆ in asb. Cem. + ½ in Gypsum Wallboard	50(2)
(xiii)	Composit 1/8 in Asb. Cem. ⁷/₁₆ in Fibreboard	20

1) No. 16 s.w.g. 1 in sq wire mesh must be fastened between the two sheets of wallboard.
2) Values shown apply to walls only.

Time Assigned for Contribution of Wood or Light Steel Frame

Description of Frame	Time Assigned to from in Minutes
i. Wood Stud walls	20
ii. Steel Stud Wall	10
iii. Wood Joist Floors and Roofs	10
iv. Open Web Steel Joist Floors and roofs	10(07)

Building Code Requirements

In many cases a building is not required by code to be fire resistive but the designer chooses to use components which resemble rated fire resistive units (or which may in fact be rated). For instance, structures recently observed in the Washington, DC area are rated as Type 3C (unprotected ordinary) under the BOCA (Building Officials and Code Administrator's International, Inc.) Basic Building Code. The floors are of bar joist construction with concrete topping on corrugated metal. The suspended ceilings need only meet Fire Hazard (flame spread) requirements. When the job is finished its appearance will be similar to a rated floor and ceiling assembly and protected with the same surface finish. Wood joists would have been acceptable under the code and the floor as installed may not be as resistive to collapse as a wood joisted floor.

In a fire investigation it may be necessary to determine whether or not a fire-resistive structure or structural element reacted to the fire in a manner consistent with its rating. This can be extraordinarily difficult. Assuming that the building was required to meet fire resistance standards, there can be several reasons for determination of the reason for failure to perform adequately. Information developed may be of use in prosecution, civil actions, code changes or fire suppression planning.

Did the building meet code requirements? This requires a thorough knowledge of code requirements at the time the building was built and access to original drawings, change orders and officially authorized variances.

Possibly, in fact, the building met modern code requirements but when given the ultimate test, the fire, the code requirements were proven inadequate. Such information, properly developed and carefully documented, is vital to translating costly experience into recommended code revisions.

Valuable information also can be developed to aid fire suppression forces in preplanning and combating future fires in the same or similar buildings. For example, the investigation may develop information that the sealant of the floor slab to the panel exterior walls was made of foamed plastic which lacks "dimensional stability" (that is, it melts). If this was permitted in one building, it may exist in other buildings built about the same time.

Involvement of Ceilings

Fires generally burn upward. Thus, the ceilings and upper parts of walls are generally exposed to higher temperatures than the lower parts of walls and floors. Fire exposed ceilings can fail early in fires, sometimes considerably earlier than a fire test rating would indicate. The fact that a particular ceiling fell may be an important element in an investigation. It cannot be assumed that the ceiling stayed in place for as long as one might conclude from its quoted fire rating.

Recently there have been a number of cases of fires burning downward (10). Many plastics when ignited form a pool of fire on the floor. The plastic may be from building contents or it may have been installed as part of the wall or ceiling.

Material falling from the ceiling may extend the fire beyond the area of origin. Consider a noncombustible building with steel bar joists with combustible tile ceiling mounted on the bottom side of the joists. There is a gap atop the masonry partition wall equal to the height of the top chord of the joist. Heated gases passing through this gap into the adjacent space may ignite the combustible tiles on their upper side. They may fall, extending the fire beyond the masonry wall.

Building Elements

Historically the chief consideration in building fire problems has been given to the Structural Elements of the building, but in building fires three elements can be identified:

- Structural Elements
- Nonstructural Elements
- Contents

The structural elements are those which are necessary to the stability of the building. The nonstructural elements may be more important in the development and extension of a fire than the structural elements. Nonstructural elements which contribute to the fire are independent of the type of construction and may be found in any of the five structural types discussed. For instance, a high flame spread interior finish of plywood and fiber tile may be found in any type building. The life hazard due to rapid flame spread over the surface will be the same. In the case of a combustible building the interior finish may be the kindling which ignites the structure. In the case of a noncombustible or fire-resistive structure, the structure will not be ignited, but substantial damage may be done to structural elements.

Nonstructural elements can include the electrical system, interior finish on ceilings, walls, and floors, air handling systems, openings from floor to floor such as shafts, stairways, interior courts, and combustible exterior surfaces and insulation.

In the majority of fires the initial fuel is the contents. Only rarely is the building directly ignited.

Interior Finish

Up to World War II there was only one significant interior finish, plaster installed over either wood lath or metal lath. It is noncombustible and, when properly installed, provides a degree of fire resistance for combustible structural elements. If the plaster is penetrated and if wood lath is present, the wood lath may provide substantial fuel.

The interior finish of the building may be the most important single element in the development and spread of a fire. In a number of cases interior finish has been a major factor in the rapid spread of fire and resultant loss of life.

Interior finish may be applied to the ceiling, walls or floors. Building codes have applied specific limitations on the flame spread classification of wall and ceiling materials. Floor coverings are less likely to be regulated but flame spread over carpeting, for example, has been an important factor in a number of serious fires. Standards and techniques for measuring carpeting flame spread have been developed recently and these regulations have begun to appear in the codes.

There are a number of ways in which the restriction of high flame spread interior finishes can be circumvented which do not appear in the code regulations. Materials which would not be permitted by the code if attached to the building may appear in significant amounts as furniture, in exhibits, as free standing office dividers, and in merchandise displays.

Alterations are sometimes accomplished without a building permit and buildings properly built have been altered with the use of high flame spread ceiling or wall materials.

Even the building permit does not guarantee safety. Consider a building with a combustible acoustical tile ceiling. It is planned to "modernize" the room by installing a ceiling grid with tiles and light fixtures mounted below the existing ceiling. A local code may require the new tiles to meet flame spread requirements but there is no requirement to remove the old combustible ceiling hidden in the void. Such a hidden ceiling can generate heat and gases which can move upward through available openings.

The investigator must try to get an accurate description of the wall and ceiling surfaces before the fire. Often only very slight clues are available, for example, nails holding scraps of furring strip to joists may indicate that there was a combustible acoustical ceiling. Adhesive beading on a wall may indicate where paneling had been secured with adhesive. Small pieces may be found behind unburned baseboard.

Table 5 contains a listing of selected materials commonly used for interior finish in buildings and a rough classification according to flame spread rating by ASTM E 84. This tabulation is intended only as a general guide and the reader should not assume that all material of the same

Table 5 Approximate Spread Raing (E-84 Tunnel Test)

Ceilings

Gypsum Plaster	0
Sprayed Mineral-base plaster	0-20
Enameled metal	0-20
Mineral fiber tile	10-25
Glass or mineral fiber bord or title, coated	10-40
Wood-base acousical tile (flame proofed)	20-75
Wood-base acoustical tile (untreated)	75-300

Walls

Brick, concrete, asbestos-cement board, ceremic tile, gypsum plaster	0
Enameled st eel, aluminum	0-20
Gypsum board, various facings	10-50
Wood, fiberboard (flame-retardant treated)	20-75
Plastic Paneling (flame-retardant-treated)	20-75
Wood, at least 0.5 in thick, various species	70-200
Plywood paneling	70-300
Hardoard	100-250
Cork	200-500
Cloth, paper, wood veneer, fiberboard (untreated)	500+
Shellac finish on wood	

Floors*

Concrete, terrazzo	0
Vinyl Asbestos Tile	10-50
Red oak	100
Linoleum	100-300
Carpeting**	50-600

---

* Use of E 84 Tunnel Test on Floor Covering Materials is no longer recommended. See other Methods, for example, NFPA 253 and ASTM E648
** Depends on type of face fiber, uunderlayment, method of attachment if glued down, loose, etc.

---

all materials of the same generic type will perform in a similar manner. Furthermore, although a flame spread classification rating or label denotes that a test has been performed on a sample of the material, there is no assurance that the material will not contribute in a major way to the spread of a fire in an actual building situation. A fire investigator should not hesitate to request that tests be performed on samples of unburned material removed from the building where the finish material appears to have contributed significantly to the fire.

In removing materials for testing the investigator should understand how the test is done so that proper samples will be obtained. If it is possible that criminal proceedings will develop, the samples must be treated as any other criminal evidence.

ASTM E 84, the Steiner Tunnel Test, is the usual basis for legal regulation of flame spread. The sample required is about 22 in width and 24 ft (565 mm x 7.32 m) in length. It may not be easy to get a sample of this size, but it may be necessary.

The fact that the method of attachment is important to the actual flame spread of combustible tiles was discovered when a full size sample of tiles glued to gypsum board showed a much greater flame spread than the same tiles, removed from the board for shipment

ASTM E 162 requires a sample only 6 x 18 in (15 x 46 cm). Samples this size is easier to get. For some materials, results from this test can be correlated in a general way with ASTM E 84 but no direct relationship should be assumed. The information developed can be useful in developing better code requirements. If the question of discrepancy in the installed material is going to be criminally significant, the prosecutor should be made aware of the difference in these tests because it might be critical to the case that the test be performed under the same conditions as the code requires, which would almost invariably be ASTME 84.

Carpeting should first be tested to the requirements of FF 1-70 (11), al so known as the "pill test". The "pill test" only measures the ignitability of the carpet from small flame sources, such as a dropped, burning match. If the carpet passed the "pill test", and it was thought to have contributed significantly to the fire, it may be useful to test the flame spread properties of the carpet, properties which are not involved in the "pill test". One flame spread test procedure is that given in NFPA 253, Standard Method of Test for Critical Radiant Flux of Floor Covering Systems Using a Radiant Heat Energy Source. For this test, samples 10 x 42 in (25 x 107 cm) are required. If a pad was used with the carpet, this pad should be included with the carpet in the test.

Nearly all carpets will spread fire if the exposure is sufficiently intense. However, some carpets spread fire under less heat exposure than others. If a pad is used under a carpet, the pad generally will cause an increase in the carpet's flame spread characteristics. The purpose of conducting the NFPA 253 test is to determine whether the carpet spreads fire easily or is more resistant to this spread than other carpets. The results of NFPA 253 will be a number called the critical radiant flux (CRF). To compare this number against other carpets, one should then refer to reference which lists the CRF's for many different types of carpets, with and without padding.

MATERIALS

Introduction

Knowledge of the effect of fire and high temperature on all types of materials -- construction, interior finish, furnishings and contents is essential to the job of the fire investigator. In searching through a burned building, the investigator should make note of the materials which were relatively unaffected as well as those which burned, charred and melted. The historical patterns of fires in buildings should be recognized and comparative differences or similarities noted.

Properties of Materials

There are many properties of materials which determine their response to fire and high temperature, as well as the contribution they may make to the growth of a fire. The principal fire properties of organic materials are heat of combustion and ignition temperature. Other thermal and mechanical properties include heat conductivity: ·specific heat (heat absorption capacity), melting and softening points, coefficient of expansion (elongation due to heating), shrinkage, cracking, etc. Some typical thermal properties are listed in table 6.

The high thermal conductivity of metals can be a means of spreading fire, for example, through sheets, ducts, joints, connectors and fasteners. Specific heat (or more accurately volumetric heat capacity) is a measure of the capacity to absorb and store heat. A material with a high heat capacity will heat up slower and may keep the maximum air temperatures lower but it will also retain the heat longer. Where high temperatures exists, thermal radiation is important and shiny surfaces (aluminum, steel, mirrors) may reflect the heat to other surfaces. While reflective surfaces would be expected to remain cooler, in most cases smoke deposition, oxidation and other changes often occur on shiny surfaces so that they eventually absorb as well as most other materials. Melting and softening points are obvious indicators of fire scene temperatures, provided allowance is made for fallen ceilings (which may protect materials at floor level), heat sinks (metals, for example, or water) and exposure to heat prior to the fire.

Classes of Materials

Masonry. In common usage, this term includes precast or cast-in-place concrete, concrete and cinder block, brick, stone, cement and clay tiles (terra cotta). Under fire exposure, many masonry walls will remain intact. However, due to thermal expansion caused by severe heating of the exposed surface (usually the interior surface), ordinary brick, block and stone walls may sometimes lean out at the top and collapse. The integrity of masonry walls depends to a large extent on the quality of the mortar bond at the joints. Collapse also may occur for other reasons, including failure of a non-masonry supporting element, thermal expansion of floors, beams or trusses, or impact loading due to collapse of a floor, a roof, another building, or an explosion. A brick veneer wall depends for its integrity on the wooden structural wall to which it is fastened. If the wooden wall is damaged, the brick wall may collapse.

Table 6 Typical Thermal Properties of Selected Materials

Materials	Density Lbs/Cu Ft	Thermal[1] Conductivity Btu-in Hr ft2 °F	Spefic[2] Heat Btu/lb °F	Percent Increase in Length for each 100°Temp Rise	Melting Point °F
Air	0.06	0.2	0.24		
Water	62	5	1.0	0.01	32
Aluminum	165	1400	0.22	0.14	1220
Brass	530	720	0.09	0.11	1650
Copper	560	2600	0.09	0.09	1980
Cast iron	440	320	0.13	0.06	2466-2550
Steel	490	310	0.12	0.06-0.15[3]	2370-2550
Glass	160	6	0.20	0.04-0.06	2600
Brick	120	5	0.22	0.05	--
Concrete, normal Weight	140	9-12	0.16-0.25	0.06-0.08	--
	120	4	0.2		
Asbestos-cement board	45	1.1	0.30-0.55	0.03-0.05	--
	32	0.8	0.33-0.45	0.02-0.03	--
Wood (oak, maple)	65	1.0	0.33	--	--
Wood (fir, pine)	35	0.8	0.29	--	--
Hardboard	15	0.35	0.30	--	--
Plywood	70	3-6	0.23	--	--
Fiberboard (wood or cane)	50-60	1.5	0.26	--	--
	0.6	0.5	0.2	--	--
Plaster	3	0.3	0.2	--	--
Gypsum Board	3	0.3	0.25	--	--
Glass fiber batt	-	1-2	0.2-0.3	0.3-1.0	--
Mineral wool	-	0.7-1.0	0.32-0.35	0.3-0.4	--
Plastics, rigid	2	0.26	0.32	0.3-04	--
Vinyls Styrene Polystyrene foam Polyurethand foam	2	0.18	0.38	0.4	--

Note: Values listed are estimated values at ordinary temperatures, or over typical temperature ranges in fires, if available.

Actual values vary considerably with temperature, particularly where moisture is involved.

[1]The number of Btu transmitted in one hour, through one square foot, one inch thick, for each degree of temperature difference.
[2]Specific Heat is the number of Btu required to increase the temperature of one pound of the material one degree F.
[3]Steel elongation increases at higher temperatures.

Concrete. Concrete is typically composed of portland cement, sand and coarse aggregate, for example, gravel, stone, cinders, slag, shale, vermiculite. The proportions may vary, for example, from 1:1:3 for columns to 1:3:6 for foundations. Concrete has high compressive strength but low tensile or shear strength. When exposed to elevated temperature under load, the compressive strength decreases and is one-half of its normal value at a temperature of about 1100°F (593°C). When exposed to rapidly rising temperatures, concrete is susceptible to spalling which is the (sometimes violent) loss of surface material. Spalling is attributed to the rapid generation of steam and depends upon moisture content (generally above 5%) in the concrete, type of aggregate and compressive load. Spalling is more likely in concrete which has not had sufficient time to lose its initial water of hydration, a process which continues for years in heavy concrete sections.

Ordinary concrete contains no steel reinforcement (or only light reinforcement). Concrete blocks may be made from cement sand and gravel, or from cement and sand alone, or from cement, sand and cinders.

Reinforced concrete is a composite mixture in which steel rods or bars are used to provide tensile and flexural strength. Fire may cause the concrete to spall away from the reinforcing steel. The strength of the concrete structural element depends upon the close bond between the steel and the concrete. Damaged concrete may be structurally unsafe. The tendons used in prestressed concrete totally lose their prestress at 800°F (427°C).

Steel. Steel has high tensile and compressive strength and is used in buildings in many sizes, shapes and products. Steel loses strength at elevated temperatures. When used as a structural member its yield, tensile and compressive strengths decrease to one-half of its normal value at a temperature of about 1000 to 1100°F (538° to 593°C). The color of heated iron and steel is sometimes used as a measure of temperature (see table 7). Steel is used in rolled or built-up members, in bar and thin sheet "C" joists, as channels, tees and angles, and as a variety of connectors such as nails, screws, bolts, hangars, and gusset plates. The fire characteristics of the steel, including high heat conductivity, substantial thermal expansion and decrease in yield strength at high temperatures, may be critical factors in a fire. For instance, a 20 ft steel member will elongate almost 2 in when heated to 1000°F (538°C). If restrained, it will buckle to accommodate the expansion. The buckling may cause structural collapse and may be well removed from the point of origin of the fire.

Gypsum. Gypsum is used both for plaster and for manufactured wall boards. Gypsum is one of the few materials which absorb heat from a fire, rather than contributing to the fire. It performs well in fires. It is widely used in fire-resistive assemblies. If the question of fire resistance is an issue, careful examination of the rear of several full sections should be made to determine if the board has a label or marking indicating it was listed by UL (Underwriters Laboratories Inc.) or FM (Factory Mutual Research Corp.). If the board is listed, then the installation should be compared with the code requirements, particularly in type and spacing of nails, cement cover over the nails, taping of all joints and firestopping of the structure.

Wood. Lumber is sawn wood used for construction purposes, although the word timber is often applied to large cross sectional pieces of lumber. Under fire exposure, wood undergoes dehydration, followed normally by a burning and/or charring process. Charred wood has readily defined layers or zones. The charring rate is roughly 0.025 or 1/40 in/min, but varies significantly with species, density and moisture content. The relatively thin wood members of frame construction may lose structural strength rapidly on fire exposure. Thick structural members may retain their strength for long periods but the structure itself may fail because of failure of the connections.

Table 7 Approximate color of Glowing Hot, Solid Objects

Appearance	Temperature °F	°C
No emission detectable	Less than 885	Less than 475
Dark red	885-1200	475-650
Dark red to cherry red	1200-1380	650-750
Cherry red to bright cherry red	1380-1500	750-815
Bright cherry red to orange	1500-1650	815-900
Orange to yellow	1650-200	900-1090
Yellow to light yellow	2000-2400	1090-1315
Light yellow to white	2400-2800	1315-1540
Brighter white	higher than 2800	Higher than 1540

Wood cannot be "fire proofed" or made "noncombustible". However, it can be treated to reduce its rate of burning by a variety of surface treatments and impregnations with mineral salts. Pressure impregnation is one of the most effective methods of reducing surface flame spread, rate of heat release and smoke generation. If there is an apparent poor performance of impregnated or surface-treated wood, samples should be removed and tested for adequacy of the treatment.

Plastics. This term refers to a group of organic substances (resins) of high molecular weight which can be shaped or molded into finished solid products. Cellulosic plastics, which include cellulose acetate, ethyl cellulose, methyl cellulose and cellulose nitrate, are produced by chemical modification of cellulose. Some plastic products are blends, combinations or composites with unique properties; some can be compounded to be thermoplastic or thermosetting. Thermosetting plastics are those which undergo chemical reaction and cure during molding and do not melt. Some thermoplastics melt at temperatures only slightly above 212°F (100°C) and may form liquid pools and burn intensely in a manner similar to flammable liquids. Examples of the two types of plastics and quoted values of service temperatures and ignition temperatures are given in table 8. These temperatures may not relate directly to actual performance of products in fires, since the test methods do not take into account specimen size, heat transfer properties, aging, etc.

The fire performance of plastics depends upon type, use and level of exposure. Some plastics form a char structure which may inhibit further burning, but most plastics will burn rapidly and generate heat, smoke and potentially toxic gases at fire temperatures. The plastics may be almost completely consumed, and the investigator should investigate for the presence of plastics in fires which reached high intensity early.

Table 8 Plastics

Typical Uses	Continuous Service Temp [1] °F	Ignition Temp [2] Flash °F	Ignition Temp [2] Self °F	Decomposition Temp Range °F
Thermoplastics				
ABS — Piping, refrigerators, telephones	175-212	--	--	--
Acrylic/Methyl Methacrylate — Glazing, light diffusers, furnishing	170-23	540-570	830-860	340-570
Cellulose Nitrate — Throwaway test tubes	120-160	285	285	--
Polyamide (Nylon) — Carpeting, clothing, appliances	180-250	790	795	590-715
Polycarbonate — Glazing, appliances, light diffusers	250	--	930	--
Polyethylene — Containers, vapor barriers	160-230	645	660	635-840
Polypropylene — Wire insulation, appliances, piping	190-280	650	730	625-770
Polystyrene — Appliances, furnishings, thermal insulation (foam)	140-175	650-680	910-925	570-750
Polytetrafluoroethylene (Teflon) — Cooking utensils, wire insulation	500	--	985	950-1000
Polyurethane — Furniture cushioning, coating, thermal Insulation (foam)	250-300	590	780	--
Polyvinyl chloride — Floor and wall covering, wire insulation, piping, Upholstery, clothing, coating	150-175	735	850	390-570
Thermosetting				
Alkyd — Paints, lacquers	350	--	--	
Epoxy — Protective coating, reinforced plastics	210	885-930	1150-1190	
Melamine — Tableware, laminates	280		900	
Phenolic — Laminates, appliances	250-350	635-750	810-910	
Polyster — Partitions (Glass-reinforced), boats	350-525	--	--	
Silicone — Electrical Insulation, coatings, grease	120			
Urea Formaldehyde — Thermal insulation				

Flame retardants added in manufacture may be used to reduce the ease of ignition and flammability of some plastics.

Insulation. The principal types of thermal insulation used in buildings are (1) mineral wool batts, blankets and fibrous loose fill, (2) foamed plastics, (3) inorganic (vermiculite, perlite) loose fill, (4) organic (wood or cane fiber) boards and (e) organic (macerated paper) loose fill.

Batts and blankets may be supplied with an integral vapor barrier (asphalt-treated or aluminum-foil-faced Kraft paper) which is intended for application to the warm-in-winter surface of the wall or ceiling interior finish board. The paper facing"is flammable and should never be left exposed. The batts are held together with a combustible binder. Plastic foam, which is combustible, should never be left exposed and most building codes require that a layer of 1/2 in (1.3 cm) gypsum board or equivalent barrier protection be provided.

Loose fill cellulosic insulation is commonly made of ground-up paper with chemicals added to reduce flammability. The more common chemicals used are boric acid, borax, and various sulfates and phosphates and these are added in amounts ranging generally from 15 to 30% by weight. If the chemicals are not added properly, they may segregate and leave portions of untreated paper. Loose fill insulation may be poured or blown into attics or blown into walls. Unless care is taken to maintain clearances around light and heat fixtures, and around flues and other heated surfaces and heat-producing appliances, smoldering of the cellulosic insulation may occur.

UTILITY SYSTEMS

Introduction

Brief descriptions of the types of utility systems found in buildings are provided. Those features and materials of the various systems which have resulted in fires and fire spread are discussed. The principal utility systems are:

1. Plumbing systems;
2. heating, ventilation, and air conditioning systems;
3. electrical systems.

Plumbing Systems

Plumbing systems include water supply and waste removal (sewage). Water supply systems, as the wording indicates, supply water to the building's fixtures and equipment. Sewage systems remove the waste products, usually accompanied by water for ease in movement, from the building.

Piping for both water supply and waste removal systems may be either metallic (copper, steel, or cast iron) or nonmetallic (plastics such as chlorinated polyvinyl chloride, polyvinyl chloride and acrylonitrile-butadiene-styrene, or CPVC, PVC, and ABS, respectively).

In some code jurisdictions, gas piping is included under the local plumbing code provisions and, as such, is a plumbing system. Piping for gas supply systems includes wrought iron (black pipe) and zinc-coated pipe (galvanized).

The major concerns with plumbing systems from a fire standpoint are with:

1. Piping, if metallic, providing an accidental ground for stray electrical currents;
2. piping, if nonmetallic, providing a fuel for nearby fires with the resultant spread of the fire;
3. penetration of fire-resistive walls and floors without proper protection (firestopping) leading to the spread of the fire;
4. leaks or ruptures in fuel gas piping and the possibility of ignition of the leaking gas.

Gas leaks have contributed too many accidental fires. The leak does not have to be within the building to pose a fire problem. Gas from leaks in the underground piping outside of a building has been known to follow the piping through the wall of the building and contact an ignition source within the structure. Also, gas leaking outside of the building has been known to have entered the sewage system and flowed back into the building through untrapped floor drains, reach an ignition source within the building and explode. Natural gas and liquefied petroleum gas have no natural odor. They are odorized artificially. The odorant may be removed as gas leaks through the earth or it may be absorbed in the scale in the inside of the pipeline. As a consequence, the absence of any reported gas odor does not necessarily mean that gas was not present. Gas leaks in the underground gas utility systems which result in accidents should be reported to the National Transportation Safety Board. While the Board must investigate any accident in which a fatality occurs, the Board also will assist in the investigation of any serious gas utility accident.

The major concerns from fire in plumbing systems are with:
(1) leakage from joints, especially in gas piping or sewer systems, where sewer wastes may produce methane; and (2) improperly constructed penetrations of fire-rated assemblies by the piping or appurtenances. Under fire exposure certain installations of plastic piping, either water or waste, may contribute to spread of fire or emit toxic gases.

Heating, Ventilation and Air Conditioning

Heating. The basic types of heating systems are hot water, steam, hot air and electricity. Hot water and steam systems utilize water usually heated by coal, gas, or oil-fired boilers. The hot water or steam is conveyed to radiators and/or convectors by piping. In hot-air systems, the air is heated by coal, oil, or gas-fired burners, or electric-resistance heaters, and conveyed throughout the building through ducts. Electrical heating systems generally utilize either radiant panels (resistance heating cables) built into the floor or ceiling or baseboard heating coils (convective panels) with electrical service supplied directly to the heating units.

Ventilation. Mechanical ventilation is provided either in conjunction with the air conditioning systems, or is in the form of ventilating fans installed in exterior walls or roofs and exhausting directly to the outdoors or into exhaust shafts which lead to the outdoors. Supply or makeup air is usually obtained through grills in doors or exterior walls, or by air leakage through openings.

Air Conditioning. There are two primary types of air conditioning: (1) central systems with distribution ducts or piping, utilizing compression or absorption-type refrigeration equipment or (2) packaged room or zonal air conditioners with free air discharge.

Central air conditioning systems utilize electricity, natural gas, or fuel oil to operate the compressors and a refrigerant as coolant in the coils and condensers. Either cooled air is circulated through ducts or chilled water is circulated through piping to individual room or zone convectors.

Individual packaged room or zonal units are generally electrically operated with closed refrigerant circuits self-contained within the units and may, depending on the conditions of usage, take fresh air from the outside or recirculate the inside air.

Heating, ventilation and air conditioning systems may be the cause of the original fire or the systems may contribute to the growth and spread of the fire. Fire initiation may include:

1. Explosive ignition due to the accumulation of gas or oil vapors within the equipment from failure of equipment controls;
2. ignition of fuel gases or oils from leaks in the piping or in the equipment;
3. ignition of combustibles near flue pipes, combustion chambers, and radiant heating units.

In air duct systems, most codes require fire dampers at points where ducts pierce fire-resistive walls and floors (where not in a shaft). In fire investigations, it is sometimes important to determine whether these dampers operated properly. As noted below, air conditioning and ventilation systems are sometimes designed to perform specific functions, such as smoke removal from the area of the fire. It is sometimes necessary for the fire investigator to determine whether such a system was installed and whether the system operated as intended.

Smoke Movement

The explanation of heated smoke and gases rising and mushrooming under the roof, if not vented, is adequate for simple structures. In tall buildings a number of factors may cause the movement of smoke to locations far beyond the area of origin, without necessarily affecting the areas in between.

Smoke movement may be caused by:
1. Thermal energy of the fire;
2. wind;
3. stack effect;
4. air handling system;
5. special built in smoke removal equipment;
6. openings in the building;
7. atmospheric conditions.

Wind. The wind exerts a pressure on one side and suction on the opposite side of the building. It may be powerful enough to overcome any of the other forces discussed here. It may change direction a number of times during the fire. It may blow in different directions at different levels of a high-rise building, particularly in congested areas where "canyon effects" may occur. The effect of the wind is increased when openings occur in the building. It is important to note that the wind at the fire may not have conformed to the information recorded at the nearest official weather station.

Stack Effect. This is due to differences between the inside and outside temperatures. The greater the difference, the greater the stack effect. Under cold weather conditions, normal air flow in the lower part of the building is from floors into shafts. The flow will decrease on successively higher floors until there is a "neutral zone", one or more floors where the flow is minimal. In the absence of wind, this generally will be from 1/3 to 1/2 the height of the building. Above the neutral zone the flow reverses, from the shafts onto-the floors, with the pressure (and thus the flow) increasing with height. The greatest flow therefore is from the lowest floors into the shafts and out from the shafts onto the highest floors. Thus top floor occupants sometimes may be the first to report a lower floor fire. In air conditioned buildings on a hot summer day, the flow may be reversed, that is downward. It should be kept in mind that the stack effect exists due to temperature difference and height. The fire does not cause it, the fire gases simply are transported by it. As an example of stack effect on fire gases, a rubbish fire on the ninth floor of a high-rise building under construction ignited PVC (polyvinyl chloride) air conditioning connectors. The fumes greatly distressed workmen on the 35th floor. They started to walk down the stairs but the stairwell was so full of noxious fumes that they got out at the 25th floor. They smashed the glass windows to get relief. This movement of gases from a lower to an upper floor was due to stack effect.

Air Conditioning. The investigator should determine the effect of the system on the fire. If the system was supposed to react to the fire in some way, the suggestions in the next paragraph are pertinent.

Special Smoke Removal Equipment In some buildings special equipment is provied to vent the fire area. It may be triggered automatically or manually. In other buildings the air conditioning system may have been designed to assist in controlling the spread of smoke.

There are two questions the investigator can ask:

"Did the special smoke removal equipment operate as designed? If it did operate as designed, were the results adequate?"

Openings in the building. Openings in the building, particularly large ones, can disrupt stack effect, multiply the wind effect, and disrupt the operation of mechanical equipment. When and why openings occurred might be important information as the fire investigation develops.

Atmospheric Conditions. When the temperature of the atmosphere is constantly decreasing as height increases, the condition is called "lapse". Under "lapse" conditions smoke will move up and away from the fire. If there is a layer of air warmer than the air below, this layer is called the "inversion layer". It acts as a roof to rising smoke. A high rise building may penetrate an inversion layer. This causes substantial differences in the smoke situation above and below the layer.

Wood-Burning Stoves and Furnaces

In recent years, there has been a growth in the use of wood-burning stoves and furnaces to provide either primary or supplemental heating. Such equipment, if not installed with adequate clearances to nearby combustible materials is potential sources of accidental fires. The burning of wood leads to the production of creosote which tends to deposit in the flue pipes and chimneys. This is particularly true of the newer so-called air-tight stoves. Operation of these stoves at low-firing rates enhances the production of creosote. The buildup of creosote in the flue pipes and chimneys can lead to a severe fire in the flue and chimney as the creosote is combustible. Flues and chimneys, be they masonry or the newer all-fuel triple-wall metal variety, should be able to withstand a total burnout. However, they may not due to deficiencies which may have been built in or have occurred with the passage of time.

ELECTRICAL

Electrical service consists of the following:

1. Service drop wires, either overhead or underground (from the public utilities' lines to the building);

2. service-entrance wires (from outside of building to equipment on the inside);

3. meter;

4. service entrance switch (to disconnect entire installation from public utilities' lines);

5. panel boards providing fuse or circuit breaker protection as well as disconnect means for each of the individual branch circuits;

6. grounding system;

7. distribution system - individual circuits, for lighting, appliance, and equipment operation.

There are six different types of wiring systems in common use. They are: (1) rigid conduit; (2) thin wall conduit; (3) flexible conduit; (4) nonmetallic-sheathed cable; (5) armored cable; and (6) knob-and-tube (which is seldom used today). Electrical codes are very specific with regard to where each of these systems may be used.

Junction boxes and outlet boxes are required at every location where wiring is spliced or insulation is removed, and at fixture locations.

In older buildings, electrical installations may have been made without outlet boxes at all splices and where insulation had been removed. In these locations, and where the wiring has been run in joist or stud spaces, dust, cobwebs and other easily ignitable materials may be present. If the splices and joints have not been properly made, there is a possibility of either short circuits or overheating of wire junctions thus leading to fire.

Another common cause of electrical fires, particularly in single-family dwellings, is the replacement of fuses of one rating with those of higher rating, that is, replacement of 15 ampere fuses with 20 or 30 ampere fuses. This practice may result in the overloading of the electrical wiring causing overheating and breakdown of insulation, and, if in close proximity to combustibles, eventually to smoldering and possible flaming ignition.

FIRE SCIENCE

Ignition Sources

FLAMING IGNITION

Introduction

Flaming ignition itself requires no explanation or definition as we are all familiar with it. The investigation is often quite straightforward when accidental flaming ignition occurs. Many fires ignited by open flames occur with people present and are either snuffed out quickly or witnesses can describe for the investigator the type of ignition, what was ignited, and how. Without witnesses, the ignition mode must be determined from available evidence.

Matches

The most common flaming ignition source is the match. Fires started with matches include: children playing with matches, careless disposal of flaming matches into trash cans or receptacles, and the use of matches by the arsonist, often combined with large quantities of combustible materials, flammable liquids, or other accelerants. Arsonists have used matches as delayed ignition devices by tucking a burning cigarette into a book of matches. Sometimes the remains of the match book can be found in the debris, including the wire staple used to fasten the matches into the cover, indicating to the investigator that the fire may have been set. The wire staple used in many book matches is smaller in size than the normally-used, office-type wire staple. The presence of the smaller staple in the fire debris, while not positive proof of a set fire, should, at least, start the investigator thinking of that possibility.

It is difficult to ignite thick materials with a match; as an example, attempting to ignite the wooden arm of an upholstered chair is almost impossible. Some intermediate material is necessary to ignite large items from a simple match. Crumpled newspapers are an excellent kindling, particularly when placed on an upholstered chair or sofa. Draperies or clothing also can serve as intermediate materials. An effective arsonist will attempt to utilize for his intermediate materials those materials normally present to avoid suspicion. The only clue the investigator may have in this situation is that the intermediate materials were not found in their normal location in the building.

Heating Equipment

Another flaming ignition source is heating equipment. This includes furnaces, boilers, stoves, space heaters, fireplaces, and their flues, chimneys and vents. Fires can originate from the escape of fuel, with subsequent ignition, ignition of nearby combustible surfaces from overheated equipment surfaces, and escape of heat or flames from flues and chimneys. Faulty operation of heating equipment or its associated controls can produce run-away fires and explosions. Unusual ignitions can occur from heating equipment long after the original installation, such as ignition of wood in contact with steam pipes after several years of exposure.

The types of heating equipment and the possible sources of flaming ignitions are so varied that it is not possible to describe all of these adequately in this book. The best that can be done is to call the investigator's attention to the large role heating equipment has in accidental fire starts. In other words, the possibility of a fire from the heating equipment, if it was operating at the time of the fire, must be given serious consideration.

In recent years, there has been a renewed interest in wood stoves for either supplemental or primary heating. These heating devices appear to be more hazardous than central heating systems. As a consequence, it is anticipated that the number of accidental fires from these stoves will be on the increase over the next several years until the consumer learns to control the hazards or the renewed interest diminishes. The point for fire investigators to remember is that if the fire scene contained an operating wood stove, be suspicious of it unless all of the available evidence points elsewhere.

Cooking Equipment

This category of flaming ignitions is responsible for the largest number of residential fires in the United States each year. However, few of these fires reach major proportions and, as a consequence, result in fire department response and subsequent investigations.

Those that do result in fire department response are generally the result of ignition of oils, greases, and fats on the cooking range. Nearly all building codes permit the installation of combustible kitchen cabinets over the cooking range. In the event of a fire on the range, there is a good possibility the cabinets will be ignited. From this point, it is only a short period of time until the complete kitchen is involved. The investigator normally has little difficulty with this fire cause as the physical evidence as to the source of the fire (pans on the burners and/or the controls in the "0W" position) is usually evident.

Other cooking equipment is sometimes responsible for fires usually due to thermostat failures in appliances such as toaster ovens, deep fat fryers and electric fry pans. Determining that one of these appliances was the cause is relatively easy, unless the fire damage is extensive. Even then a history of problems with the appliance may be uncovered in interviews with witnesses.

Electrical Equipment

Electrical equipment, which would include some of the appliances under "Cooking Equipment", is covered in chapter 4.4 and will not be discussed here.

Other Flaming Ignition Sources

Many open flame devices are used in the construction of buildings, such as salamanders for heating and torches (now, usually propane) for sweating pipe joints in copper plumbing. These, and other open flame sources, have been responsible for many fires in buildings under construction. The plumber's torch is a particularly frequent ignition source due to the nature of the operation. A typical story goes like this: The plumber is sweating a fitting in the common bathroom wall between two apartments on the first floor of a two-story apartment building. The wall is insulated (for noise reduction) with paper-wrapped, fiberglass batts. The plumber places a piece of sheet metal behind the fitting to keep the torch flame off of the batts. He is having difficulty seeing what he is doing as the electrical circuits have not been completed. The plumber is working away when all of a sudden he sees a flame emerge from behind the sheet metal and race up the paper into the wall of the floor above before he can stop it. The fire extends into the attic and burns off the roof and 16 apartments on the floor above before the local fire department can contain the fire.

Fires caused by cutting and welding operations also are fairly frequent. Three problems are inherent in these operations of which the investigator should be aware. First is the torch itself. Careless handling of the torch can cause ignition of nearby combustibles. Second is the sparks and hot slag resulting from the cutting or welding. These may fall onto nearby combustible materials, start smoldering fires of which the welder is unaware, and later, after everyone has left the premises, and break out into flames. Third is the transmission of heat through the metals being worked on resulting in ignition of combustibles in contact with the reverse side of the metal. This latter problem is particularly frequent in shipboard repair work.

Reference

Highlights of the National Household Fire Survey, National Fire Prevention and Control Admin. Dept. of Commerce (US) (no date).

SMOLDERING COMBUSTION

Introduction

In some fires, the first material to ignite exhibits a non-flaming slowly propagating combustion. Similar behavior is often observedt after the flames have diedt as glowing embers. Both are examples of smoldering combustion. This deep-seated combustion process consumes fuel very slowly with the leading edge or front generally moving at rates about one inch per hour. As a result, it generates relatively little heat and small quantities of combustion gases compared to flaming combustion. The danger lies in the nature of these gases and in the difficulty in detecting smoldering before it changes to a flaming mode.

Ignition by Smoking Materials

For home one of the major reported sources of destructive fires is the glowing cigarette, often igniting trash accumulations, bedding or upholstered furniture. Carpets, curtains, draperies and other items are less frequently involved.

Literally hundreds of billions of cigarettes are smoked each year in the United States. This means that every minute of the day hundreds of thousands are being lit, smoked, and discarded. Fortunately the vast majority of these "smokes" are successfully extinguished. The time required for an unpuffed 3.3-inch (8.4-cm) cigarette to burn its full length (in air) in a horizontal position is approximately 20 minutes. However, if the cigarette were to burn on a piece of interior furnishing (such as a mattress, chair or sofa) covered by a piece of clothing, newspaper, etc., it may smolder for 45-60 minutes before burning its full length. Typical tip temperatures may reach 1100°F (593°C).

The fuel must be porous to be ignited by a smoldering cigarette. Once ignited, the heat decomposes more material to form a porous char and volatile gases. Air slowly diffuses through the pore structure to the hot smoldering front. There the char reacts with the air to give some carbon dioxide, carbon monoxide and enough heat to continue the combustion. The char structure is critical to smoldering in other ways too. It is an effective insulator, so that the small amount of generated heat is not dispersed. It also maintains the open maze through which air continues to diffuse to the smoldering front. Should the char collapse, melt or produce tarry material which blocks the pores, the smoldering would cease. For these reasons, most common plastics do not smolder.

However, most upholstered furniture (chairs, sofas, etc.) and mattresses are made with cover fabrics and porous stuffing materials whose ignition temperatures (500-700°F, 260-370°C) may be easily exceeded by burning cigarettes. Some upholstery cover fabrics resist cigarette ignition better than others. Wool, nylon, olefin, polyester, and various other synthetic plastics generally melt rather than smolder. Cotton, rayon, linen, and blends of these fibers (cellulosic fabrics) will ignite from burning cigarettes and smolder. Leather will smolder and silks will not.

Filling materials used in upholstered furniture and mattresses consist of cotton batting, urethane foam, foam rubber and polyester or combinations of these. Of these, cotton batting and foam rubber can easily be ignited by burning cigarettes. Urethane foam and polyester will melt under the heat of a cigarette and usually will not ignite. However, under certain circumstances, urethane foam covered by upholstery fabric can be ignited (smolder) and even burst into flames. Such an occurrence might take place in a crevice of a chair or sofa where a foam cushion abuts a vertical side arm. A smoldering cigarette in this location may easily start a fire.

Whether a cover fabric is cellulosic or synthetic (plastic) may be determined by applying a match to a sample of the fabric and observing whether it melts, chars or flames. If on extinguishing the flame a glowing persists, then the fabric is cellulosic (cotton, rayon, linen, or blends). If the fabric melts and drips, it is synthetic, for example: polyester, olefin, or nylon. Wool will not sustain combustion from a low heat source and will give off a pungent odor similar to the smell of burning human hair.

In filling materials, cotton batting is easily identified as is polyester fiberfill. Determining whether a foam material is rubber or urethane can be accomplished by a simple match test that is, by ignition of a small piece, extinguishing and smelling the odor of residual smoke. The two classes of materials give off distinctive and different odors, and the identity of the sample at hand can be obtained by comparison with known foams. If these are not available, foam rubber will smell of burning rubber and polyurethane foam will have a "sweet" odor.

Hazards of Smoldering

Three hazards are associated with smoldering combustion. The first lies in combustion products. The smoke is produced slowly. Even at this slow rate, dangerous gases are being generated. The slowly diffusing oxygen sees vast active fuel surfaces. This excess of carbon promotes the formation of noxious carbon monoxide over the less dangerous carbon dioxide. During the long alarm delay, the toxic gases accumulate and may be responsible for incapacitation and deaths, even before there is major damage to the premises.

The second danger lies in the eventual transition to flaming combustion. Char temperatures in cotton, for example, can exceed 900°F (482°C), well above the fire point of the volatile gases being "boiled off" ahead of the smoldering front. Higher surface temperatures and the accompanying higher volatilization rate can result from even small increases in the air movement across the smoldering area. This brings oxygen (air) to the smoldering fuel at a higher rate. This, in turn, increases the char burning, raising its temperature, which in turn, pre-heats more fuel faster, producing more gases and char at an ever-increasing rate. Should the concentration of these gases exceed their lean flammability limit, a sudden eruption of flames would result.

The third danger arises when uninformed persons try to extinguish smoldering fuel. Often the fire appears to be extinguished, the material is not removed to a safe location, and a serious fire breaks out later. Deep-seated combustion is very well named.

Analysis of the Fire Scene

What can one look for to determine whether a smoldering ignition began a fire? Unfortunately, if the fire flames, the post-fire scene will be the same as after an initially flaming fire. The accounts of witnesses to the fire may be helpful, particularly if they remember smelling smoke for some time before the fire was discovered.

If the fire goes out or is suppressed before flaming begins, the evidence will be more obvious. Look for a partially charred mattress or chair. Since relatively little soot is generated, note the cleanliness of the walls. The soot deposition or wall charring should be slight and localized near the source. (If flaming occurs, soot deposition will be extensive.) Smoldering will rarely ignite flammable fluids or solids which are not in direct contact; thus their continued presence is an indicator. Lastly, because the smoldering propagation is so slow, the ignition source, such as a cigarette or electrical fixture, should be obvious to the careful investigator.

SPONTANEOUS IGNITIONS

Introduction

Spontaneous ignition, formerly called spontaneous combustion, has been widely used to classify the apparent ignition and burning of material without the external application of heat, spark or flame usually considered necessary for ignition. In most cases the term spontaneous is misleading. Many prefer the term "self-heating" or "self-ignition" and these terms often will be found in the literature. These terms also may be somewhat misleading since heating and ignition, if they occur, are usually dependent on both special storage conditions and the introduction or presence of chemical or biological material, which is necessary if the process is to occur.

Spontaneous ignitions are spontaneous only in the sense that flames suddenly appear on the surface of a previously nonflaming material. The conditions leading to this flaming are usually lengthy ones involving the build up of heat within the material over periods of hours, days, months or even years in some instances.

There are some exceptions to this statement. Some very reactive or pyrophoric materials may produce flames almost immediately when exposed to oxygen or another chemical with which a rapid reaction can occur. Such ignitions occur on the surface of the reacting material and thus can occur in periods of a few seconds or less. These materials normally require special handling in the industrial plant or laboratory.

Ignition leading to flaming requires the generation of heat at a rate faster than it can be lost to the surroundings. This is an especially important requirement if a material is to self-heat to a state where ignition is possible. Thus, almost all cases of spontaneous ignition require that the material involved be in bulk form which, in itself, comprises a thermal insulator. The outer portions of the material thus form an insulating layer and serve to prevent rapid heat loss from the central core. Of course, the size of the material bulk which can self-ignite will be a function of its coefficient of thermal conductivity, its thermal reactivity, the temperature of the surroundings, and the degree of convective cooling around material.

Self-heating may occur in materials for a number of reasons: (1) the material may be unusually reactive at normal temperatures, (2) normally inert materials may become activated through additives either during bulk storage or prior to it, (3) biological action may raise the temperature to a level at which the material itself can start reacting, and (4) stowage of hot material can result in self-heating to ignition even though the same material stacked in the cold condition shows no evidence of self-heating.

The exact nature of self-heating has not been clearly defined. As suggested above, it may vary with the type of material and/or the stimuli required to initiate the heating process. In almost all instances, the process is possible because of the nature of thermochemical reactions.
If a pile of material starts reacting at normal temperatures, the insulating effect of its outer layer limits heat loss to the surrounding air. Temperatures build up in the center of the pile with the outer portions acting as a thermal insulator. Thus, spontaneous ignition starts by heating up and usually charring the interior of a pile of material prior to any discoloration of the outer surface.

Self-heating materials have been known, in the early stages of the process, to release odors, smoke and perhaps have slightly elevated surface temperatures. If the pile of self-heating material is opened or split down the center, the center of the pile will be found to be hot, discolored, or charred, depending on the length of time the process has been in progress. If, after opening the pile, it is both hot and charred, there is great danger that rapid ignition will occur, quickly involving the bulk of the material. Because of this, it is much safer, if the pile is large; to probe the pile with a thermometer or thermocouple to determine whether self-heating is in progress. On the assumption that the material storage temperature conditions have been reasonably constant for a considerable prior period, the absence of temperatures within the pile significantly above the previous storage temperature indicates no self-heating

Occurrence

Biological Initiation

Perhaps the most common occurrence of spontaneous ignition used to be that of hay which had been incompletely dried prior to bulk storage in barns. The moisture present allows biological action to take place. The heat release from this action can raise the temperature within a bulky and well-insulated pile of hay to a temperature of 167-176°F (75-80°C). At this point biological action is destroyed by the heat. This temperature, however, is high enough to permit, under some storage conditions, continued heating of the pile resulting eventually in a fire. Such fires were reasonably common when hay was stored in bulk form. With the introduction of baling equipment, resulting in storage of hay at much higher density, spontaneous ignition has been less frequent. Since spontaneous ignition of hay is well known, this cause is often assigned. It is important that the unburned pile not be disturbed until the investigator can examine it. If there is no evidence of heating within the pile, spontaneous ignition is not the cause.

Chemically-Reactive Materials

Another common cause of spontaneous ignition is the oily rag. Unsaturated vegetable oils absorbed on cotton waste or rags can readily self-heat and ignite. A list of these oils in approximate order of sensitivity from high to low reactivity is as follows:

1) Linseed;
2) tung;
3) hemp;
4) poppy seed;
5) sunflower seed;
6) tobacco seed;
7) soybean;
8) corn;
9) cotton seed;
10) rape seed;
11) castor.

These materials combine with oxygen from the air, releasing heat in the process. Their adsorption on cotton or other fiber can greatly increase the surface-to-volume ratio through which this oxidation can occur and, thus, increase heat release per unit volume. If the oil soaked rags or fabrics are wadded up in a large ball, the heat liberated will be conserved and ignition may occur. If, on the other hand, the rags had been suspended from a line in one or two layer thickness, rapid heat loss to the air would prevent ignition. Cargo nets and empty sandbags, treated with oil for preservation, also have been known to ignite spontaneously when stored in piles.

Some of the oils previously mentioned were commonly used in paint and varnish manufacture and numerous fires have been blamed on improper storage of oil-soaked rags. This type of accidental ignition has been greatly reduced by the introduction of latex paints, commonly used today.

Note that all of the above oils are vegetable. Petroleum oils, as found in garages, do not ignite spontaneously. This difference in behavior between vegetable and petroleum oils is not well recognized. Sometimes fires are attributed to mineral-oil-soaked rags by persons who may be attempting to misdirect the investigation.

Both wood and coal appear to be sufficiently reactive to self-heat and ignite under conditions which conserve the generated heat. In most cases, though, these conditions involve very large piles, a more or less open structure such that air can penetrate the pile and an extended period of time. It is not likely an investigator will frequently encounter fires in which self-heating of coal is a possible cause. As a consequence, the self-heating of coal will not be discussed.

Initial Heating of Material

Materials safe at room temperatures can present spontaneous ignition hazards if stored in piles while at elevated temperature. For instance, both cellulosic fiberboard and glass fiber insulatinn material have been shown to self-heat when stored in large piles direct from the production process. This problem has been recognized and standards now require the cooling of the material below a temperature of 140°F (60°C) before bulk shipment of the cellulosic fiberboard. When spontaneous ignition is suspected, it is necessary to consider the circumstances along with available physical evidence. An accidental fire in a clothes dryer load may be thought impossible since the heat level of normal clothes drying is too low to produce ignition of cloth. Examination of the evidence, however, might reveal the presence of foam rubber garment pads. Foam rubber is a material, which, when heated to moderate temperatures, can ignite spontaneously.

Like foam rubber, polyurethane foam can become self heating after being heated to moderate temperatures. Polyurethane foam "buns", freshly manufactured, are isolated for a period of time to cool or to permit safe ignition, if ignition should occur.

Pyrophoric Metals

Some metals are pyrophoric in that these metals can ignite spontaneously in air under certain circumstances. These metals include plutonium, uranium, thorium, zirconium, hafnium, magnesium, calcium, potassium, and sodium. The conditions which will produce ignition vary widely from metal to metal. Liquid sodium will react violently when dropped into water. Urani urn scrap will ignite spontaneously, parti cul ar.ly under summer heat conditions, if not stored under oil or water. The subject of spontaneous ignition of metals is a complex one. If spontaneous ignition of metals is suspected as a possible cause of a fire, the investigator should seek the best technical advice available. Reference (7) gives a good description of pyrophoric metals.

Material Tests for Spontaneous Ignition

If the fire investigator needs to determine whether a material may have undergone spontaneous ignition, there are several test methods which can be used to measure some aspects of self-heating behavior. However, as the services of a laboratory will be needed to conduct these tests, the investigator will need to seek assistance from qualified laboratories

Summary

Numerous unwanted fires have undoubtedly occurred as a result of spontaneous ignition. Attempts to assign this as a cause are not often successful. The evidence is often destroyed before the fire is discovered. The fire investigator should remember that spontaneous ignition, in the sense discussed here, is always a process of heating from within. Unless this can be shown, assignment of spontaneous ignition as a cause of the fire is dubious.

www.ingramcontent.com/pod-product-compliance
Lightning Source LLC
Chambersburg PA
CBHW081816300426
44116CB00014B/2383